Critical Praise for *Jerusalem Calling by Joel Schalit*

S0-AEA-574

*Selected for *Publishers Weekly* "Best Books of 2002" list

"This remarkable collection of essays by an astute young writer covers a wide range of topics . . . [and] provides an overview of contemporary critical, radical thinking . . . This is the debut of a new and original thinker."

—*Publishers Weekly*, starred review

"The essays combine provocative political analysis and a powerful first-person voice. Schalit's artful blending of the personal and the political is bound to make some readers uncomfortable. But it's also what makes *Jerusalem Calling* so good."

—*San Francisco Bay Guardian*

"Over time Schalit has risen to the forefront of a new leftist culture that's postmodern and ultra-aware but still believes in the power of activism."

—*SF Weekly*

"*Jerusalem Calling* delivers thoughtful, passionate analyses of subjects including the religious fundamentalism of American cultural politics, the failures of the left, the inner conflicts of punk, and the past, present, and future of the Arab-Israeli conflict . . . Schalit's meditations on a recent journey to Israel are more refreshingly insightful than most any other current writing on the Middle East."

—*Clamor*

"Joel Schalit's passions are unrestrained but his arguments are impeccable, his attitude distinctive. He has a clear eye for nuance and subtext, and a sharp scalpel for hypocrisy and pretense. You will hear a lot from and about this writer in the future, so be smart: get in on the ground floor. Jerusalem is calling and we all have to answer from the cell phones in our minds and hearts."

—Danny Schechter, author of *News Dissector*

"Schalit's anticapitalist, Jewish, postpunk perspectives on the Middle East, the relevance of rock music, and the true impact of religion in America pack a powerful punch, yet resonate with fellow feeling."

—Booklist

"A thoughtful collection of essays."

—Rain Taxi Review of Books

"It's a palpably vulnerable and excruciatingly honest read, and a compelling milestone in American public intellectual life."

—XLR8R

"Schalit successfully utilizes his diverse background to articulate a persuasive and progressive view of the modern world. Schalit is a thinker of our times . . ."

—The Stranger

"Joel Schalit is a model punk. Outspoken and revolutionary yet levelheaded, he has channeled his wild intellectual energy toward the pursuit of organized rebellion. *Jerusalem Calling* [is] an amazingly readable collection of essays focusing on his politics, ideology, and heritage as a Marxist, a secular Jew, and a Zionist."

—Portland Mercury

ISRAEL

VS.

UTOPIA

ISRAEL
VS.
UTOPIA

BY **JOEL SCHALIT**

AKASHIC
BOOKS

All rights reserved. No part of this book may be reproduced, stored in a retrieval system, or transmitted in any form, by any means, including mechanical, electronic, photocopying, recording, or otherwise, without the prior written consent of the publisher.

Portions of this book were previously published by Allvoices, France 24, the *Guardian*, *Tikkun*, and *Zeek*. A condensed version of *Israel vs. Utopia*'s second chapter, "Everything Falls Apart," is available in the collection *Righteous Indignation: A Jewish Call for Justice*, edited by Rabbi Or N. Rose, Jo Ellen Green Kaiser, and Margie Klein (Jewish Lights Publishing, 2008).

Published by Akashic Books
©2009 Joel Schalit

ISBN-13: 978-1-933354-87-3
Library of Congress Control Number: 2009922937
All rights reserved

First printing

Akashic Books
PO Box 1456
New York, NY 10009
info@akashicbooks.com
www.akashicbooks.com

For Jennifer

TABLE OF CONTENTS

ACKNOWLEDGMENTS

Every book takes awhile to will itself into being. Some gestate longer than others, especially when you work a full-time job as an editor. Though it may seem like an ideal space to get work done—during the time of this book's writing, I held down editorial gigs at three separate periodicals and edited three books—depending on how much consideration your subject demands, it's more likely that the actual writing will take a lot longer than you ever could have imagined.

To that end, I cannot thank my publisher, Johnny Temple, enough, for waiting as long as he did for *Israel vs. Utopia* to finally materialize. Johnny, you've been a mensch, as always. And then some. The same goes for Akashic's managing editor, Johanna Ingalls, and editor Ibrahim Ahmad. You all have been wonderful, supportive, and unbelievably patient with me. I'm thrilled to still be working with you after eight years. New York publishing still has nothing on you guys.

I'm equally grateful to this volume's editor, Charlie Bertsch, for guiding *Israel vs. Utopia* to publication. He not only handled the grammar and content with remarkable ease, but also used this project as an opportunity to teach himself about the painful reality of the Arab-Israeli conflict. My religious colleagues would call Charlie a "righteous Gentile." All I can say is that Charlie's tireless efforts made for a far better book. That, to further indulge the native, is its own mitzvah.

Heartfelt gratitude goes to Ron Nachmann, one of my favorite music critics and the former associate editor of XLR8R. Also a self-described Israeli American, Ron read this manuscript at several different stages in its development, and gave it a fabulous copyedit in its next-to-final version. Even better, along the way we discovered that Ron's father dated a relative of mine in Haifa during the 1950s. Ron, we could have been brothers. Not that we aren't already.

There are few designs as predictable as those which grace the covers of books about Israel. Whether consisting of a panoramic shot of Jerusalem or an image of an Israeli soldier, they tend to look the same. But designer Courtney Utt spent days creating a key exception; the cover is brilliant and inspired, just like the rest of her work.

My eighty-eight-year-old father, Elie Schalit, deserves a remarkable amount of credit for talking through *Israel vs. Utopia*'s main themes with me. Our conversations are littered throughout these pages, giving them a distinctly familial vibe that contributes to the intensely intimate feel of this book's subject matter.

I'd also like to thank several others: my fellow editors and friends at *Zeek*, Jo Ellen Green Kaiser and Shai Ginsburg; Arthur Neslen, Vance Galloway; and former *Ha'aretz* translator Robert Rosenberg, may he rest in peace. All of you provided invaluable comments on the articles and editorials that served as this book's basis. An equal but decidedly different form of thanks goes to the Old Jerusalem Restaurant in beautiful San Francisco. The salat Turki and knafe are positively utopian.

Angry
I said you make us angry
Angry people
That's who we are
—Keith Hudson, "Nuh Skin Up"

INTRODUCTION

Purple. Pink. Green. Orange. The brightly colored, flat-roofed, concrete residential buildings immediately stood out. No more than three stories in height, some still under construction, they could have been found in any Palestinian or Israeli Arab town, albeit one crossed with a United Colors of Benetton ad. I imagined that it could even have been a picture of one of the communities lining the highway between my parents' home and Afula. If you weren't familiar with such scenery, you might very well have assumed that this was a typical eastern Mediterranean Arab municipality.

The image in question was a promotional photograph for a London art exhibition, Occupied Space 2008: Art for Palestine, showcasing new paintings and photography by Palestinian and British antioccupation activists. Overshadowed in local media by the opening of an equally significant exhibit of contemporary political art from China at the Saatchi Gallery, the show had received a small but favorable preview from the progressive British weekly, the New Statesman. Given the subject matter, I knew I had to go see it.

An altered photo of a Palestinian refugee camp by Ramallah artist Yazan Khalili, the print had an alien quality that was perfectly suited to making a political point in this foreign context. Of course these buildings would appear differently. They were out of their element. The colorizing was intended to compel the viewer to look closely at something he or she might have otherwise taken for granted. (To wit, the same piece—from Khalili's "Camp" series—was titled "Color Correction" in a '07 collection, *Subjective Atlas of Palestine*.) Having just moved back to the UK after emigrating in 1979, I imagined I was being asked to see Palestine anew, through local eyes.

The walk between the Earl's Court tube station and the Qattan Foundation gallery did little to persuade me otherwise. First, there were the Arab restaurants lining each side of the street serving halloumi, Turkish coffee, shawarma, hummus Beiruti, the ever-popular meze platters. Then there was a bilingual Arabic/English real-estate agency sign, followed by a curiously Israeli-looking blue and white advert for a dentistry office featuring Arab-named oral surgeons. Even more interesting was that the sign listed the nationalities of the dentists next to their Arabic last names: Denmark, Sweden, and, finally, Slovakia. For anxious Jewish rightists, who believe Europe to be a hotbed of Islamic extremism, this would seem like a nightmare come true. Here, listed on a piece of commercial signage in central *Londonistan*, to cite the title of journalist Melanie Phillips's fear-mongering book about London's Islamist-inspired decline, was testimony to the degree of Europe's transformation by immigration from the Muslim world.

In musing on this curious sign, I allowed myself to conjecture how the most reactionary members of the Jewish American community would respond to being placed in such a radically mixed cultural environment.

Everywhere they'd look, they'd see only the enemy. This fear has become an inescapable feature of Jewish American life since the terrorist attacks of September 11, 2001, and one which contradicts every aspect of my childhood experiences in Israel and, subsequently, in a London in which nearly half my elementary school classmates were from greater West Asia. I had come halfway home, so to speak, to the place where I had first learned what it means to be Jewish—by living in a community with Muslims.

It is important to clarify my use of the term *halfway* here. Even though the United Kingdom is physically closer to Israel than the United States, it has always stood in my mind, while living in America, as being halfway. Not just because it is the place where I have changed planes for the last two decades between San Francisco and Tel Aviv (my parents moved back to Israel in 1994), but because it is a place in which the Middle East and Europe have, however problematically, come together to form what has been provocatively dubbed by some as "Eurabia," a new Europe in which nearly 4 percent of the region's population is of either Muslim or Arab descent.

Yet the Europe of my childhood was always the Eurabia that is now becoming fashionable in mainstream discourse. It was Eurabia because we had moved to London from Tel Aviv, and we considered ourselves to be a part of it—in contrast to the European Jews with whom we had little or no contact with, who regarded themselves as locals, not Middle Easterners. It was to this Europe that, while writing this book, I returned in the fall of 2008 with my wife, hoping that we would find ourselves more in sync with life there than we had in the United States during the final months of the Bush administration.

Truth be told, the America we had left was beginning to look far more like the Eurabia that we imagined ourselves headed toward. My home for the previous twelve years, San Francisco, had been transformed during that period. Already multicultural, with a mixture of recent immigrants and families with long histories there, San Francisco came to feel increasingly like a city in the Old World, with a density of otherness recalling places like New York and Chicago before it. More specifically, signifiers of the Middle East proliferated to an unprecedented degree.

In our neighborhood of Bernal Heights, for example, we could easily walk to at least three places to buy fresh hummus, and, during our last year there, we could even find za'atar pita stocked at the supermarket. Taking my dogs out for their evening walk, I would spy any number of bumper stickers related to the Arab-Israeli conflict: Hebrew-language stickers urging Israel not to return the Golan, hopeful designs combining the blue and white colors of Israel and the red, white, and green ones of its Arab neighbors, and blunt declarations in English to *Free Palestine*. I would regularly overhear Arabic and Hebrew being spoken on the streets, and there were even National Guard recruiting advertisements in Arabic, aimed at the area's growing immigrant population.

Serving as the editor of Allvoices, an international news portal during my final year in the city, I found myself in a workplace where talk inevitably turned to media outlets from the Middle East: the Qatari broadcaster al-Jazeera, the Israeli newspaper *Ha'aretz*, and the myriad blogs and newsletters sprouting throughout the region. Our goal was to assimilate as much as we could from all of them, as though they offered the best examples of success for us to emulate during a time of crisis in America's troubled news business. The metaphor was not lost on me. Adding to my sense that the United States had moved much closer to the region was the fact my employers were Pakistanis.

When we worked with tribal journalists from Pakistan's lawless frontier with Afghanistan, the Federally Administered Tribal Areas, Allvoices' management advised me to conceal my ethnicity from them. Initially, this upset me. Over time, though, as I learned more about the politics of that area, I came to realize that it made sense to defer to their wishes. The wisdom of the request could not have been more forcefully driven home to me later in the year when Pakistani guerrillas conducted a terrorist attack in Mumbai, India, singling out Jews and Israelis for hostage-taking and death. As the events unfolded, I made a point of keeping up with Diaspora Jewish and Israeli news coverage, wondering whether this attack might have something to do with Israel's increasingly intimate military relationship with India. Israeli arms sales to New Delhi were at an all-time high. Israeli advisors were helping train Indian forces in counterinsurgency tactics in the disputed Kashmir territory. An Indian military delegation was even visiting Israel during the attacks.

The harrowing reality of what happened in Mumbai reinforced a lesson from my childhood, showing once again the dangers that confront Jews outside of Israel, even in a historically welcoming place like India, the crown jewel of Israeli hippie culture. From the crematoriums of Auschwitz to the raves of Goa, life in the Diaspora hadn't changed as much as I had hoped. In this context, I thought it significant that no one seemed willing to highlight the parallels between the 1972 kidnapping and murder of Israeli athletes at the Munich Olympics and the events in Mumbai; Indian Special Forces, like their German predecessors, had failed to rescue the Jews they were charged with protecting. Indeed, given many Jews' predilection to see Islamists and jihadis as inheritors of the Nazi legacy—or, more dramatically, to regard the entire Muslim world as a reincarnation of Germany in the 1940s—I had expected the media to at least invoke Munich. This glaring oversight pissed me off, reminding me that, despite my commitment to secularism and diversity, I still had the political reflexes of a postwar Jew.

The tendency to see Europe in the Middle East, and, as I noted earlier, to see the Levant in Europe, conveys one of the core themes of this book: that the Middle East has become a metaphor for the world. Whether you chalk it up to undue Zionist influence on post–World War II American foreign policy, the disproportionate impact that the Arab-Israeli conflict has wielded over Western political life, the growth of Islam in Europe and Arab immigration everywhere else, or the global impact of Persian Gulf petrodollars, the point is ultimately the same: for a variety of reasons, the Middle East has become more tightly enmeshed in the West than ever before. The jihadi terrorist attacks of 9/11 and the military occupations of Iraq and Afghanistan during the War on

Terror have had the ironic consequence of colonizing American culture and politics.

Israel vs. Utopia analyzes this change from the perspective of an Israeli American who, having been raised in Israel, the United States, and Europe, finds that they all have much in common despite the repellant "othering" of Israel that takes place in the latter—even by Israelis themselves. If the West has infiltrated the Middle East, and vice versa, then how could Israel, one of the chief conduits for this transformation, remain something so thoroughly unknowable? Particularly given how many of its citizens, especially those with centuries-old backgrounds in Europe, continue to live abroad. The best answer I can provide is one that, instead of issuing a prescription, seeks to outline a struggle to know Israel better. Specifically, I want to consider and complicate the relationship between the misconceptions of Israel that flit about in fantasies of the place, whether positive or negative, and what I call, with a nod to the Cold War Left, "actually existing" Israel.

My desire to reform American understandings of Israel is significant in this regard, because so much of today's anti-Islamic invective in the U.S. is purported to be "pro-Israeli." When I hear such talk I consistently perceive a racist conflation of my national and religious identity, as though what defines my Jewishness is its inherent opposition to someone else's religion. To be pro-Israeli, to be pro-Jewish (whatever either of these things really mean), is not the same thing as being prejudiced. Unfortunately, making that equation is the easiest way to assign a specific politics to being Jewish, a fact which conservatives both in Israel and the United States have regularly exploited. Under such circumstances, Israelis like me have difficulty finding any ideological freedom of movement. And pressure from Diaspora Jewry only makes matters worse.

The negative reaction that many Israelis tend to have when Americans act as though Israel is solely reducible to its religious character illustrates a larger tension between the two peoples. Americans are able to "construct" Israelis in this manner because of the unequal relationship between the two countries. In return, Israelis typically respond as though they are colonial subjects straight out of central casting, consistently rejecting being defined by their unofficial "parents" in such a biased fashion. But they are also aware that this feeling of colonization brings them uncomfortably close to acknowledging Israel's treatment of the non-Jewish population within its own military aegis. If pressed, most Israelis will admit that the settlement enterprise in the Occupied Territories is a textbook colonial endeavor. The implications of that realization, though, pose psychological problems for a people raised on the conviction that they are always on the brink of being at the mercy of hostile forces.

Hence my title, *Israel vs. Utopia*. First dreamed up six years ago, at the depressing height of the al-Aksa Intifada, when I was living in my old apartment in San Francisco's Richmond District, it forced me to imagine scenarios where the cold, hard facts permitted only the continuation of the status quo—a problem many progressives confronted during the Bush administration—and to do so without having to determine what that utopia should be. Given how certain many people in my circles had become about Israel, their impressions hardening into reflexes, I thought there might be some benefit to suspending the impulse to draw conclusions. If Israel had become the most popular global synonym for dystopia, I reasoned, why not tease out the negative space of that assumption?

By setting Israel in opposition to what it's supposed to be, by creating a framework in which it is possible to substitute "America" or "Europe" for "utopia"—or even "settlements" for "Israel"—I wanted to restore movement to the discussion of its past, present, and future. Certainty has its appeal, but it also has a way of cluttering the mind with obstacles to reflection. Where the concept of Israel is concerned, what we need right now is room to maneuver. My hope for this book is that it will contribute to that worthy cause, helping to break up the blockages that have impeded the peace process, whether specific to the post–9/11 era or dating further back in the history of the Middle East.

Joel Schalit
July 2009
Milan, Italy

CHAPTER ONE

MY EGYPTIAN PRESIDENT

It felt like a dream. I was watching President Bush introduce the November 2007 Annapolis Conference on C-SPAN. But I could have sworn I was a boy sitting in my parents' former home in London. I had been transported back in time, and instead of President Bush, I was fixated on the spectacle of Egyptian President Anwar Sadat addressing Israel's parliament thirty years earlier.

I heard my father behind me shouting, "But he's a brownshirt!"* in reference to former Israeli Prime Minister Menachem Begin, who was playing host to the event. The idea that a right-winger like Begin would permit Israel's nemesis to speak in the Knesset had left him dumbfounded. My stepmother Esther was there too, talking on the phone to a friend. She sounded exasperated, repeating over and over in Hebrew, "Bemet, Rut . . . ha Aravit, Sadat, hu be ha Knesset!" ("Really, Ruth . . . Sadat, the Arab, is in parliament!") But Ruth didn't seem convinced. The absolute truths of our nation's turbulent history had suddenly been revealed as relative. If this could happen, what might be next?

I rubbed the sleep of nostalgia from my eyes. No, I

*During the 1920s and '30s, the Sturmabteilung (Nazi paramilitary force) wore brown shirts. For many years, the term "brownshirt" was used as a synonym for fascists.

wasn't in London. The man on my TV screen was a different sort of nemesis, one who the people of my other
homeland, the United States, had voted into office for
a second term in 2004, despite ample evidence that he
was well on his way to becoming one of the worst presidents in the nation's history. And the unnerving sense of
possibility that had resonated through my parents' voices
that stunning day of November 20, 1977, had turned into
the weary conviction that hope was too much to hope
for.

Still, it was clear that something inside me wanted
to remember a past that would make the present seem
less grim. Despite the hostility I harbored toward President Bush, I yearned for a temporary détente. I didn't
believe for a moment that he had Israel's interests at
heart. But the parallel between 1977 and 2007 was too
apparent to miss. Both speeches followed a decade of
bloodshed: Sadat's address came after both the major
Arab-Israeli wars of 1967 and 1973, and nonstop fighting
between Israelis and Palestinians from Tel Aviv to Munich during the intervening years; Bush's address came
amid a comparably vexing sequence of events—Israel's
1999 withdrawal from its security zone in southern Lebanon, the al-Aksa Intifada that began in 2000, and the
second Lebanon war of 2006.

This isn't to imply that the events of the last decade
mirror the ones that led to Sadat's successful 1977 trip
to Jerusalem, because they don't. No matter how much
I might have wanted to find hidden historical patterns
that tie these two time periods together, I couldn't. A
peaceful outcome to the present strife along the lines
of 1979's Camp David Accords remained highly unlikely,

and even if President Bush were to have brought one about, it would have been very different from the agreement President Carter helped broker between Begin and Sadat.

No, my imagined connection between 1977 and 2007 was based on a superficial and erroneous analogy—the sort that psychoanalysis teaches us to discern in dreams—between Bush and Sadat. Despite Bush's insistence throughout his presidency that strong support for Israel must lie at the foundation of America's Middle East policy, I still wanted to perceive him the way I remembered Sadat—as a former foe seeking to make peace with Israel. After all, despite Bush's steadfast declarations of support for Israel, his administration's strategy in the Middle East had done more damage to the nation than Sadat at his most belligerent.

This realization troubled me throughout the 2007 Annapolis Conference. Although it had been convened to restart the work of peacemaking between Israel and the Palestinians, I couldn't shake the impression that, because its stated goal was so obviously lacking in credibility, it was really an attempt to reconcile Israel with the United States. That was what I found so interesting about the event and why, unlike a lot of my fellow analysts, I was not willing to take a position on its declared purpose. To me, it was clear that the conference was about something else entirely.

It was with considerable bemusement, then, that I watched my colleagues argue with each other about how to react—as though formulating the proper response, whatever that might be, was as important as the mission of the conference itself. *Do we support it, despite the fact that we don't like Bush? Do we boycott it because we don't trust Bush?* So conditioned had they become to the disappointments of the peace process that, taking its futility for granted, they had stopped thinking about the reality of the conflict. Instead, many in the media worried about staking out the correct position on the inevitable failure of the latest talks.

I've grown exceptionally tired of this cynical posture. It only leads to the dead end of intellectualism, in which writing precisely calibrated editorials takes the place of working for real change. Americans, in particular, appear to take comfort in the reinforcement of familiar roles that events like the Annapolis Conference bring about. Even if they disagree vehemently with the policies of the current Israeli or American governments, they welcome being confirmed in their political and professional identities through these kinds of rituals.

The lack of meaningful progress during Bush's years in office compelled me to adopt another kind of disposition to events of this sort. The Annapolis Conference was interesting, but for entirely different reasons than the pronouncements made there or the threadbare journalistic conventions that framed them. I solicited opinions from friends, read countless wire reports, and watched as much video footage of the conference as I could, until I felt that I had something worthwhile to say. When it finally came, it wasn't what I had expected.

I realized that what mattered most to me were my concerns about Israel's lack of independence from the United States, especially evident during the 2006 Lebanon war, when the notion that Israel might be a proxy for American interests in the Middle East came into play more than ever. In hosting this conference, the United States was no longer the distant mediator it had been in 1979 when Carter brokered the first peace agreement between Israel and Egypt, nor even the nation tasked with enforcing Iraq's infamous no-fly zone and simultaneously hosting repeated peace talks between the Israeli government and the PLO in the early 1990s. No, this was a United States that had gone local, one that had finally become a part of the Middle East. The Iraq War had transformed the United States into one of Israel's neighbors. American investment in the Middle East—which has conditioned Arab-Israeli relations since colonial Great Britain and France largely pulled out of the region in the 1960s—was now grounded in a physical proximity to Israel, which, unlike the limited military force that occupied Lebanon in the early 1980s, had lost the aura of temporary engagement.

This crucial change in the region's political landscape combined with my personal history to shape a fundamental intuition: Israel can't make peace with its neighbors unless it first makes peace with the United States. Having spent my entire life split, both literally and psychologically, between the two countries, my demand for reconciliation has reached a fever pitch. As the child of a man whose family was among the first to settle in Palestine in 1882—predating not just the creation of Israel but also the British colonial authority that came before it—I have no choice but to live and breathe Israel.

Yet I am no less an American. Although she spoke to my dad in French half the time, my mother, whom my father first met as a child in Jerusalem, was as much a product of New York as my father is of Tel Aviv. I spent a good part of my adolescence and most of my adult life in the United States. For me, dual citizenship isn't merely a by-product of my Jewishness, but a condition that defines my outlook on the world and punctuates my identity as a self-described Israeli American. Whether the divide between Israel and the United States is augmented or diminished, I feel every change as a fluctuation in my soul.

MASH DOWN BABYLON

Writing this book has posed a huge challenge for me. So many people have gotten Israel wrong that the demand to get it right is almost unbearable. But the more I worked on this project, the more I came to realize that the only way to get it right is to stop trying to "get it" at all. Reality always has a way of eluding our grasp. In the case of Israel, though, the problem is absurdly magnified by the fact that the reality of Israel is, in large measure, a projection of fantasies, both by those who want to love the place and those who are consumed with hatred for it.

It's not helpful, particularly for someone like myself, that the United States remains the standard for building a nation from scratch. From John Winthrop's image of a "city upon a hill" through the idealism of the Founding Fathers, the prehistory of American politics was dominated by the desire to realize a dream, regardless of what stood in its way. Indeed, the dispossession of North America's native peoples seems like a perverse model for Israel's development. Had the territory of either the United States or Israel been empty prior to their settlement, the two nations might have succeeded in their aspirations to become places of true liberation. But the fact of those people who saw no reason to voluntarily abandon their ancestral homes made it impossible.

We all know this. Just as the most blindly patriotic American knows deep down that the U.S. exists because it displaced the people who had lived there before the conquest, every Israeli knows that his or her country could never have come into being without making room for its citizens at the expense of the area's longtime residents. Anyone who tells you otherwise is lying. The question is what to do with this knowledge.

Because Israel's sixty-plus years of existence have fallen within the era of mass media, it's commonly believed (particularly within the Diaspora Left) that its misdeeds can still be undone, in much the same way that iconographic racisms of this period—segregation in the Southern U.S., the apartheid regime in South Africa—were dismantled. The difficulty, of course, is the ultimate reach of such desires. Only the lunatic fringe claims that the United States should be returned to preconquest inhabitants. But a great many people advocate that Israel be reduced in size, if not outright erased, to make up for the suffering of the Palestinians it has displaced.

No matter how irrational, this impulse to turn back the clock still colors the discourse of otherwise sensible individuals. This isn't surprising, since it echoes the nineteenth-century Zionist dream of transforming time into space, as if the physical geography of Palestine could compensate for the destruction of the homes that stood there thousands of year before. In a way, some dream of a pre-Israel Palestine in the same way that others dream of a pre-expulsion Israel. Of all the paradoxes that haunt the Middle East today, this one may be the most poignant.

It's crucial that we pay close attention to these dreams in all their nuances when we tackle the subject of Israel, even as we recognize their fundamental perversity. There's no going back, because no matter how much some of us might want to, we're still propelled into a future filled with the rubble left behind by our dreaming. When we try to make such dreams reality, we refuse the existence of people whose presence renders those dreams impossible. True hope lies in worldviews that don't reduce human beings to the status of underbrush that must be cleared away before starting afresh. Forgetting the lesson of the Holocaust sullies the memory of the millions of lives it took—and that applies to everyone with a stake in the future of Israel, regardless of their history.

Where Israel is concerned, real progress demands that we hold tightly in check any impulse to refuse the existence of a given group of people. People, whatever their origin, are not in the way. They *are* the way. Banal as that may sound, like some slogan from a UNICEF card, it remains the only political philosophy that upholds the promise of true freedom. For though Martin Luther King Jr. called it his "dream," he knew all too well that it represented the reality that people would grasp if they could only be woken from the nightmare of history.

GOING BACK TO MOTHERLAND

While it's no longer fashionable to seek the truth in our fantasy lives, I'm convinced that we limit our definition of what matters at our peril. My conflation of Bush's Annapolis address with Anwar Sadat's visit to the Knesset, reality-based or not, helped me realize what I might otherwise have overlooked: although the physical territory of the United States is thousands of miles from Israel, the two countries had become more "neighborly" than ever before. In the wake of the U.S. invasion of Iraq, it wasn't simply American money and weaponry that now populated the Middle East, but a large military force (and its civilian auxiliaries that had been there for years).

Throughout the following chapters, I move back and forth between the sort of analysis that a historian or journalist might produce and a self-analysis more akin to intellectual autobiography. I do this not only because—as in the case of my Annapolis daydream—I sometimes get further by following my intuition rather than the "objective" information provided in news reports, but also to model a way of thinking about Israel that's become all too rare in this era of entrenched positions and strident rhetoric. If we're to break the ideological stalemate that chains both Israeli and Palestinian futures (not to mention their American counterparts), we must learn to see ourselves in the way we see others, even when it's uncomfortable or embarrassing to do so.

This reflection is especially helpful for thinking about the relationship between Israel and the United States. As I've already suggested, the two nations are bound together by their shared history as promised lands. From the beginning, both nations have been torn between the desire for renewal that led to their founding and the resistance posed by the facts standing in the way of that dream. The religious persecution that prompted early American colonists to cross the Atlantic may pale next to the abuses Jews have faced over the course of European history. But the Puritans, Catholics, Huguenots, and other Christian sects that sought refuge in what would become the United States shared with Israel's founders the conviction that their faith could only survive if there was sufficient political will to protect it. Whether they aspired to create a theocracy or its opposite, they all recognized the need to mind the role of the state in religious affairs.

Because I spent my undergraduate and graduate years reflecting on religion in the modern world and devoting much attention, as both a writer and a musician, to the rise of the Christian Right in the U.S. during the 1980s and 1990s, I'm particularly attuned to the way Americans think about Israel. But my regular visits home to Israel to see my family, and the journalistic work I've done over the years there, consistently remind me that the pull of the United States is as strong in Israel as it is amongst American Zionists and Israel's newest so-called friends, Evangelical Christians. This reciprocal attachment exists for many reasons, not least due to the flow of money between the two countries. But its foundation is psychological. Because the U.S. and Israel were both imagined long before they could be realized, neither has successfully freed itself from the realm of abstraction. The two nations are in fact haunted by their failure to transcend fantastical origins.

I know from personal experience how effortlessly conversation about Israel can slide from the literal to the figurative. While Israel is as real as any other place on the map, the fact that it was conjured during a time when it literally had no place emboldens both its friends and enemies to treat it as a trope. The "Israel" invoked in reggae songs and the "Israel" invoked in think-tank white papers are far closer to each other than most people realize.

My goal for this book is therefore twofold. On one hand, I want to reflect on how Israel figures in contemporary political discourse. On the other, I want to pull back the curtain on the reality of Israel by showing what that discourse leaves out. I can't stop Israel from being used as a figure of speech—it makes no sense to try—but I'd like to make it easier to see when and why Israel is used that way. While we may still invest the name with hopes and fears, we can better understand that those constructions originate in a concrete reality rather than an otherworldly realm in which we're powerless to intervene.

Even though this is first and foremost a book about Israel, it's also about the United States. The special relationship between these two nations invites a scrutiny that moves beyond the nuts and bolts of political and economic policy. As I hope to show, perhaps the best way to rethink Israel is by rethinking the United States at the same time.

Boxing Up Bush

The week of January 19, 2009, was a momentous one in American history. On Monday, the nation celebrated the birthday of Martin Luther King Jr. On Tuesday, Barack Obama became the first African American president. And on Wednesday, he rapidly moved to put his own stamp on domestic and foreign policy, seemingly intent on undoing most of what George W. Bush had

JOEL SCHALIT & 35

wrought during his final months in office. Even though I was living in London at the time, the historical significance of this conjuncture was still keenly felt in the predominantly Caribbean neighborhood of Brixton where I rented an apartment. Whatever would transpire in the months ahead, with the global economy on the verge of collapse, it became clear that the political consciousness of the American people—and, indeed, beyond the nation's borders—had been powerfully transformed. The message of King's famous speech from the 1963 March on Washington, in which he articulated the dream of a nation where the country's inhabitants would be judged by the "content of their character" rather than the color of their skin, might not have been achieved completely—but it no longer seemed like a shot in the dark.

Not surprisingly, the feelings of hope stirred up by Obama's improbable success in the 2008 presidential race had many of us, both within the United States and abroad, eager to move forward instead of looking back. Obama himself had repeatedly articulated this desire, even to the extent of implying in the weeks leading up to his inauguration that he was not keen on seeing the Bush administration held accountable for its perceived misdeeds. However honorably motivated, though, this was a perilous impulse. Regardless of whether it would prove fruitful to pursue the Left's long-simmering desire to see criminal charges brought against Bush, Vice President Dick Cheney, and other White House officials, it was crucial to make sense of the past eight years, lest we continue unwittingly down the path they had laid for us.

It is no accident that the Israel Defense Forces' incursion into Gaza, heavily protested in Europe and the United States, came to a halt on the eve of Obama's assumption of the presidency. Whatever other motivations Israeli leaders may have had for launching their assault, the timing of the attacks indicates that they were desperate to use political capital that might no longer be available after Bush vacated the White House. While many commentators indeed noted that they were taking advantage of a lame-duck American president, the quid pro quo nature of this action went largely unnoticed. To those few experts on Israel not blinded by their own feelings, it was obvious that Israel was redeeming credits it had earned by reluctantly accommodating the Bush administration's agenda in the Middle East. In other words, the concentrated force of the assault on Hamas and the Palestinian civilians who were unable to flee from its strongholds was another legacy of the Bush era.

Although it is never easy to put recent history in perspective, the scope of that legacy has proved particularly difficult to comprehend. George W. Bush's detractors are fond of claiming that he was one of the worst presidents in American history. Yet unlike the predecessors to whom they typically compare him, such as Warren G. Harding and Franklin Pierce, Bush accomplished a great deal while in office. The statement he made in his last presidential address—that he had been willing to "make the tough decisions"—was an attempt to remind everyone that his term had been defined not by hesitancy but activism. And, for better or worse, he was right. For the most part, though, it was a message that people were unwilling to hear. In their eagerness to break new ground, they failed to acknowledge the degree to which the Bush administration reshaped the entire political landscape.

If this is true wherever the Bush administration intervened, from its refusal to sign the Kyoto Protocol to its radical curtailment of domestic civil liberties, it is particularly obvious in the Middle East. Even if Barack Obama were to make good on his campaign pledge to pull American troops out of Iraq as rapidly as possible, the long-term effects of their presence will last for decades. Simply put, the presidency that so many people are practically willing themselves to forget is one that we must force ourselves to remember. For my part, the insight that Bush was not really the unequivocal friend of Israel that he claimed to be, but rather an enemy of its best interests, is one that I worked hard to sustain in the heady first days of the Obama administration. In this regard, it is important to think critically about the way that the 2008 presidential campaign was received in Israel, for the perceptions formed then, while the Bush administration still held sway, are bound to condition the relationship between the United States and Israel in the years to come.

OBAMA MEANS MUSLIM IN HEBREW

By the time Barack Obama locked up the Democratic nomination to run for president in June 2008, the relationship between the United States and Israel was shaping up to be of unprecedented significance in the American political process. Despite Obama's effort to cultivate the impression that he was as pro-Israel as the next Democrat, the suspicion that he might bend where previous American leaders had stood firm still permeated the Jewish community. All manner of rumors circulated about him: He was a Muslim. He was part of Chicago's large Palestinian community. He was a leftist bent on punishing Israel. He was beholden to an African American community notorious for its anti-Semitism. He was a foreigner who wanted to undermine the United States from within.

Not coincidentally, these were the same rumors being spread on the Right. The fears articulated by Jewish voters, particularly among senior citizens, mirrored the sort of comments being floated by conservative talk-show hosts like Rush Limbaugh, Sean Hannity, and Laura Ingraham. To an unprecedented degree, their brand of hyperbolic conjecture was being targeted at a community that had long been a pillar of the Democratic Party. And, in the weeks during which she refused to concede the nomination to Obama, Hillary Clinton seemed to have no qualms about letting the attention being paid to Jewish voters work to her advantage. For a good while, it seemed as if the resistance they expressed toward Obama's candidacy might help derail his campaign for president.

Because Barack Obama ended up winning 78 percent of the Jewish vote, outperforming John Kerry's 2004 results in many places, and won the crucial swing state of Florida with surprising ease, liberal political analysts breathed a huge sigh of relief. Many made arguments about how the loyalty of traditionally Democratic Jewish voters was far more steadfast than Republican strategists had realized. What these optimistic assessments overlooked, however, was the highly unusual combination of circumstances that helped propel Obama into the

White House. Had the price of petroleum products not skyrocketed and then collapsed, had the stock market not plunged precipitously, had the housing crisis been contained, had terrorism loomed larger in the autumn news, Republican nominee John McCain might well have prevailed. As a number of conservative commentators noted, Republicans had faced a "perfect storm" in the campaign and still managed to avoid the sort of landslide defeats experienced by Democrats like Walter Mondale and George McGovern. From this perspective, Karl Rove's contention that the United States remains an essentially conservative nation may not be mere wishful thinking.

Similarly, in the aftermath of the election, many of Obama's cabinet nominations and the comments he made about international affairs in general (and the Middle East in particular) suggested that he remained acutely aware of how close he came to being defeated by wild rumors about his identity and motives. It was telling that upon taking the oath of office on the same Bible that Abraham Lincoln had used, right-wing conspiracy mongers immediately claimed that the massive book was a Koran. Even if Obama had wanted to reprimand Israel for its incursion into Gaza, political prudence demanded that he move forward without paying the assault too much attention. Just as the nation's financial crisis had limited his freedom of movement on domestic policy, Obama's political autonomy had been sharply restricted by both the Israeli offensive and the Bush administration policies that had, in effect, inspired it.

It is important to be mindful of the fact that this quandary was not only the product of the Bush administration's previous policies, but of a specific effort to put Obama on the spot. In his May 15, 2008, address to the Knesset in celebration of Israel's sixtieth anniversary, Bush went out his way to develop the Republican Party line that the McCain-Palin ticket would later deploy in the fall:

> *Some seem to believe that we should negotiate with the terrorists and radicals, as if some ingenious argument will persuade them they have been wrong all along. We have heard this foolish delusion before. As Nazi tanks crossed into Poland in 1939, an American senator declared: "Lord, if only I could have talked to Hitler, all this might have been avoided." We have an obligation to call this what it is—the false comfort of appeasement, which has been repeatedly discredited by history.*

Although careful not to name Obama directly, Bush's clear allusion to statements the candidate had made early in the Democratic primary season about being willing to talk with the leaders of countries like Iran and North Korea was powerfully reinforced by the example of that "American senator" who had so laughably underestimated Hitler. Obama responded accordingly, calling out the president for his veiled attack, only to have the Republican nominee, Senator John McCain, pick up Bush's lead in response.

The problem was magnified by the fact that even after it had become clear that she couldn't secure the Democratic nomination, Hillary Clinton kept reminding people about the demographics where she had polled far better than her opponent, including within the Jewish community. Thus, Obama had his work cut out for him when he addressed the annual meeting of the American Israel Public Affairs Committee (AIPAC), the most influential pro-Israel organization in the United States. Predictably, he went through the same motions as so many candidates before him, indicating that he was firmly committed to maintaining the special relationship between the United States and Israel, and would use military action to do so when necessary.

The speech was by most accounts very well received, despite the earlier skepticism circulating in the audience. But that didn't prevent formerly Democratic Senator Joseph Lieberman—according to some accounts John McCain's first pick for a running mate—from trying to steer anxious Jewish voters in the direction of the presumptive Republican presidential nominee. The point of contention was Obama's forceful assertion that Bush administration policy in the Middle East had actually weakened Israel's security:

> I don't think any of us can be satisfied that America's recent foreign policy has made Israel more secure. Hamas now controls Gaza. Hezbollah has tightened its grip on southern Lebanon and is flexing its muscles in Beirut. Because of the war in Iraq, Iran—which always posed a greater threat to Israel than Iraq—is emboldened, and poses the greatest strategic challenge to the United States and Israel in the Middle East in a generation.

Rather than explore the possibility that Obama was sincerely articulating a new way for the United States to support Israel, Lieberman was content to echo the charge of appeasement that Bush had made to the Knesset. "Iran is a terrorist, expansionist state," the Jewish Telegraphic Agency quoted Lieberman as saying, confirming that the political shorthand of the Republican Party line was still in sync with its Israeli counterpart. Interestingly, although the Jewish Telegraphic Agency's story gave Lieberman's point of view, it also provided enough content to refute it:

> *"This is a new approach," said Steve Rabinowitz, a Democratic consultant whose communications firm also does work for many Jewish organizations. "Two years ago many thought it would be difficult to persuade people that George W. Bush had not been good for Israel, even dangerous to try it. It's not only a case that can be made now, it's also true."*

In retrospect, Rabinowitz's confidence seems to have been justified, given Obama's performance among Jewish voters. Despite the constraints he was operating under, it appeared that Obama wanted to make it clear that he would not simply pick up where the Bush administration had left off with regard to American-Israeli relations. During the process of selecting his cabinet and formulating policy objectives, he consulted with liberal Jewish peace advocacy organizations such as Brit Tzedek v'Shalom, J Street, and the Israel Policy Forum. That he also talked with the conservative groups that have historically served as the "voice" of the Jewish community, such as AIPAC and the arch-rightist Zionist Organization of America, however, indicated the caution with which he had to proceed. While those groups had suggested to varying degrees that Obama would be no friend to Israel, he lacked the standing to leave them out in the cold. Still, the fact that the Obama team was listening to anyone beyond the usual mouthpieces was of note, even though many liberals in the U.S. remained skeptical that his selection of Hillary Clinton as secretary of state would lead to any fundamental changes in American foreign policy.

While it makes sense that Israelis of all political preferences would prepare for the possibility of a shift in American policy, the positive attention given to the idea of a "new approach" suggested a willingness in both Washington and Jerusalem to rethink the rituals of the special relationship. Besides, even the pro-Israel bias displayed by the Clinton administration was, at its worst, more engaged in the effort to create some kind of solution than the Bush administration. As a left-wing Israeli peace activist once told me, "For all of the horrible problems with Clinton's approach, in retrospect, it may have been better for Arafat to have accepted it all, and stage another intifada later, because at least he would have been working with more than the Palestinians will start with when the next round of peace negotiations inevitably are forced upon them."

THE POLITICS OF BOREDOM

The day before President Bush addressed the Knesset back in May 2008, he spoke at Israeli President Shimon Peres's first annual Facing Tomorrow Conference. Three quarters of the way through his talk, Bush's mouth seized up, as though he were about to say something important that he just couldn't figure out how to put into words. I waited and waited, but the expression remained on his face. My computer had frozen.

This is Bush's moment of truth, I chuckled to myself, *the moment that he realizes his failure to say anything new*. It was hardly the first time I'd had a laugh at the president's expense. Although progressives around the world were reduced to a meager diet of hope in the seemingly interminable years of his leadership, we were also able to sustain our spirits on empty calories of irony. It wasn't satisfying fare, to be sure, but still preferable to the grim alternative of submitting to the status quo. Even with a speech in hand, Bush seemed to be rendered functionally speechless by his administration's failure to make any concrete progress in the Middle East. His now-notorious landing on a U.S. Navy aircraft carrier in May 2003 to declare "Mission accomplished" had come to stand for his entire presidency.

Unlike the Anwar Sadat of my imagination, Bush had declared war, not peace, in Israel's chief legislative body—and not on Israelis, but on the leading contender for his successor, Barack Obama. Bush acted that day as though Israel's parliament was American territory, implicitly comparing Obama to appeasers like Neville Chamberlain, the late British prime minister who had attempted to pacify Hitler by allowing him to invade Czechoslovakia. Despite the drama, Israeli Prime Minister Ehud Olmert exemplified the overwhelming sense of tedium during Bush's address by nearly dozing off, while Deputy Prime Minister Eli Yishai shifted around in his seat like a bored and impatient school kid. Although the speech provided comfort to Jews, both in Israel and the United States, it was the sort of comfort that accompanies sleep, not action.

When my father shouted, "But he's a brownshirt!" back on November 20, 1977, he was expressing amazement that Menachem Begin—a fiery religious nationalist who advocated the concept of a "Greater Israel" stretching from British Mandate–era Palestine to the Occupied Territories and what is today Jordan—could break with precedent. The hope his exclamation conveyed in the process—that change can be brought about by the peaceful initiatives of individuals rather than the collective sacrifices of war—was largely abandoned in the waning years of the second Bush administration. Yet that hope shows signs of returning in the willingness of Barack Obama and other Democratic Party leaders to push for a new approach to the problems of the Middle East, despite facing significant political risk in doing so.

CHAPTER TWO

EVERYTHING FALLS APART

They've lost control of the debate," historian Tony Judt told the *Observer*'s Gaby Wood in February 2007, discussing the Jewish American organizations that had worked to marginalize his criticisms of Israel. "For a long time all they had to deal with were people like Norman Finkelstein or Noam Chomsky, who they could dismiss as loonies of the Left. Now they're having to face, for want of a better cliché, the mainstream: people like me who have a fairly long established record of being Social Democrats (in the European sense) and certainly not on the crazy Left on most issues, saying very critical things about Israel."

Although Judt spoke confidently, the rancor generated by his outspoken statements on the subject of Israel had clearly affected him deeply. Earlier in the interview, he explained how a talk he was scheduled to give at the Polish consulate in New York the previous October, entitled "The Israel Lobby and U.S. Foreign Policy," had been cancelled at the last minute due to pressure from those same groups that—though they may have lost control of the debate—still had the power to restrict where it could take place. "They do what the more tactful members of the intelligence services used to do in late Communist society," Judt remarked of the Anti-Defamation League. "They point out how foolish it is to associate with the wrong people. So they call up the Poles and they say: did you know that Judt is a notorious critic of Israel, and therefore shading into or giving comfort to anti-Semites?"

The possibility of being classified as one of those "wrong people" has increased markedly for commentators like Tony Judt over the past decade, as well as for Jews who would once have been exempt from such labeling. Whereas organizations like the Anti-Defamation League once concentrated their efforts on professed anti-Semites, they now seemed more preoccupied with finding Jews who claim not to be anti-Semitic while fostering support for anti-Semitism. Although Judt's analogy between such organizations and the enforcers of totalitarian states is compelling, they might be more aptly compared to the Red-hunting of the McCarthy era. What people like Judt have experienced is an attempt—however muted its public expression—to blacklist.

That's why the Jewish press in New York referred to the controversy over the cancellation and its aftermath as "l'affaire Judt," conjuring the late-nineteenth-century Dreyfus affair in which a French officer of Jewish descent was accused of treason. The fact that over 100 intellectuals (many of whom disagreed with Judt on key points) found it necessary to sign an open letter of protest on his behalf underscores the significance of an episode that under other circumstances might have attracted little attention.

Published in the November 16, 2006, edition of the *New York Review of Books*, the letter excoriated the Anti-

Defamation League for working behind the scenes to have Judt's talk canceled, and then denying its role in the affair. "In a democracy," the letter declares, "there is only one appropriate response to a lecture, article, or book one does not agree with. It is to give another lecture, write another article, or publish another book." The letter's conclusion underscores the gravity of the situation, noting that despite the many differences of opinion held by its signatories "about political matters, foreign and domestic, we are united in believing that a climate of intimidation is inconsistent with fundamental principles of debate in a democracy."

Predictably, the Anti-Defamation League's National Director Abraham Foxman answered the letter with outrage, also in the *New York Review of Books*, complaining that its coauthors Mark Lilla and Richard Sennett had not bothered to get the organization's side of the story before going public: "What is so shocking about this letter is that a group claiming to be defending fundamental values of free expression in a democratic society—values that ADL has worked to ensure for decades—employs techniques which completely debase those values." Although Foxman was aware that some of the letter's signatories, including Lilla himself, could hardly be considered progressives, his reply nevertheless managed to artfully conjure the specter—rooted in the student radicalism of the 1960s—of a Left more intolerant than its antagonists. "Their behavior is a much subtler and more dangerous form of intimidation than the baseless accusations conjured up against ADL."

The most striking part of both this exchange and l'affaire Judt generally was its lack of civility. The speed with which each side resorted to implicating the other in totalitarian tactics clarifies how threadbare the sense of common identity and purpose had become within the Diaspora by the mid-2000s. Whereas previously one could have imagined heated debates about Israel cooling off into the impression of solidarity, in this case any resolution seemed impossible. In a sense—to play off of Judt's formulation—everyone *had* lost control of the debate. The American Jewish Committee raised the stakes even further when they published an essay by Holocaust scholar Alvin Rosenfeld asserting that the position on Israel held by Judt and other progressive Jews like American playwright Tony Kushner and British literary theorist Jacqueline Rose is functionally anti-Semitic. Suddenly everyone in the Diaspora seemed to be talking about issues that in the old days no one wanted to discuss.

In his *Observer* interview, Judt explained to Wood that this reticence had been secured by fear: "All Jews are silenced by the requirement to be supportive of Israel, and all non-Jews are silenced by the fear of being thought anti-Semitic, and there is no conversation on the subject." Though it seems deeply ironic that the fear of more vigorous silencing would inspire people to speak freely, this shift is one that Judt—a former translator for the Israel Defense Forces—clearly welcomed, concluding the interview on a hopeful note: "I think one could say that after the Iraq War, for want of a better defining moment, the American silence on the complexities and disasters of the Middle East was broken. The shell broke and conversation—however uncomfortable, however much slandered—became possible. I'm not sure that will change things in the Middle East, but it's changed the shape of things here."

For better or worse (or, more precisely, for better *and* worse), discussion of Israel has shifted markedly in the wake of the attacks on the United States of September 11, 2001. Trends that began to emerge at the conclusion of the Cold War are now fully manifest. As l'affaire Judt amply illustrates, rancor has supplanted reasoned exchange as the dominant mode of discourse. Even when people are on the same general side, they find ways to treat each other as opponents. The polarization of the debate has made people who want to find solutions despair of making progress. But it has also provided an opportunity to rethink the way Israel is regarded both within its borders and beyond. What we need in the midst of all the heated polemics on Israel is a way to perceive the gray in both black and white.

That's my primary goal here. I want to bring depth to conversations that have been flattened into reflex. In this chapter and the ones to follow, I focus on specific examples from recent debates in the media. Frequently, I connect them to the history that preceded them. But this is not a history book. What concerns me, as I suggested in my introduction, are not the facts of modern Israel's existence, but the way people have marshaled those facts in the service of polemics, whether in the United States, Europe, or the Middle East. Although denouncing arguments for their rhetorical sleights of hand may feel good, it does little to advance the cause of peace. Just as it becomes harder to generalize about members of a particular ethnicity or religion when you get to know some of them personally, it's more difficult to judge positions in a debate after you study them in depth, with as much attention to their nuances as their broad strokes. But that's a challenge I take up eagerly, as the only way for us to make progress in an ideological debate is to challenge our certainties.

PREOCCUPIED TERRITORIES

Visiting New York in February 2007, I got into a conversation with a Jewish gentleman in his sixties who wanted to discuss what Israel had achieved in the Six-Day War of 1967. Because I was born in that year and grew up in a context where Israel's stunning victory remains so crucial to understanding contemporary Jewish attitudes toward the country, I'm always eager to talk about it, and have become accustomed to Americans rationalizing the necessity of the occupation, in one form or another, as a means of ensuring Israel's security, as though they were justifying the defense of their own country. But what this man said unsettled me more than usual. He only seemed able to countenance the war's impact on American life.

Israel's transformation into a state with military muscle and the imperial conquests to prove it was significant, he explained, because it completed the process of Jewish integration in the U.S., helping us secure the level of equality we experience in America today. From his perspective, what the Six-Day War meant to Americans outweighed the changes it caused in the Middle East. The war cleansed the Jewish American population of the stigmas it had borne, and was evidently worth the stigmatization that the occupation of formerly Arab lands had ultimately inflicted on both Israelis and Palestinians. It's hard to imagine a purer example of the figure of Israel taking precedence over "actually existing" Israel.

One of the biggest issues confronting Jews today is the way Israel gets "constructed" by both its proponents and opponents in America. When Tony Judt explained that he wasn't sure whether the controversy that Jewish critics of Israeli policy in the United States have provoked "will change things in the Middle East," but that "it's changed the shape of things here," he made a revealing comment about Israel's role in American political life. It seems that Israel has become a staging ground for conflicts that, while bearing on its special relationship with the United States, are first and foremost internal struggles. The same goes for debates about Israel elsewhere within the developed world, particularly Western Europe. But given both the size of the Jewish community in the U.S. and the extensive media network devoted specifically to its concerns, the intensity and scope of those struggles is frequently magnified within an American context.

This helps explain the vehemence with which some fellow Jews have attacked people like Judt. Even if he is right that debates within the American Diaspora may not directly impact Israel, the belief that they *could* matter elevates the significance for their participants. And when liberal journalists like Philip Weiss write about the formation of a new Jewish Left, as he did in a blog entry for the *New York Observer* on February 7, 2007, they only add fuel to the fire. Acknowledging that U.S. organizations like Jewish Voice for Peace still have a relatively small amount of influence, he found sufficient evidence to assert, "The formerly marginalized progressives are movin' in." This kind of analysis is typically sustained by a healthy dose of wishful thinking that reflects both progressives' thirst for an expanded profile and journalists' professional desire to perceive a balance of powers within the ideological conflict over Israel. But when repeated often enough, Weiss's analysis has the capacity to transform its exaggerations into reality. Once the Diaspora Jewish Right feels sufficiently threatened, it'll respond in a way that produces precisely what it fears. That's the ironic state of affairs that Judt had in mind when he declared, "They've lost control of the debate."

It's also what prompted Dan Sieradski, in an entry he posted to his former abode, the progressive blog Jewschool, to make the bold leap of calling this ideological struggle in the Diaspora a "Jewish civil war." Although Sieradski was skeptical of Weiss's claim that a unified Jewish Left was making its presence felt—implying that this "movement" only appears like a coordinated force to its opponents—he argued that progressives should aspire to such a goal. While Sieradski admitted that this wasn't likely to happen, he insisted that the outcome of his "civil war" would determine the future of world Jewry, whether fought by one army—the Zionist Establishment—or two.

Sieradski's peculiar fusion of sober realism and incendiary idealism—there is no unified Jewish Left, and yet we need a unified Jewish Left to make the "Jewish civil war" a fair fight—shows how difficult it is for members of the Diaspora to rein in the sense of self-importance that animates their ideological moves. If you see yourself as a soldier in a war that will determine the fate of millions,

you're bound to be at least a little politically and culturally myopic. No matter how pure their motives, those
who get caught up in events like l'affaire Judt end up
behaving much like those who act out their private lives
with role-playing games—eventually the distinction between fantasy and reality starts to blur.

Remember, They're Americans

Or so I would tell myself during my years as the managing editor of *Tikkun* magazine, one of the most influential
and controversial Jewish publications to come out of the
progressive Diaspora. Both my childhood in the Middle East and Europe and conversations with my family
helped put the ideological struggles between American
Jews over Israel that I encountered while working at the
magazine into proper perspective, if only because the
Israel of my upbringing seemed so much more tangible
than the abstraction I would later encounter. To put it
bluntly, they reminded me not to make mountains out
of molehills. But that's hard to remember when your attempts to close an issue of the magazine keep getting de-
layed by the angry outbursts of individuals who haven't
yet had their worldviews decentered.

Because my position exposed me to a steady flow
of vitriol, many of those rants blur together. But a few
stand out, whether for their extremity, absurdity, or
both. I remember one time when the latest issue of *Tikkun* had only been on newsstands for two days, and negative reactions from our readers were already starting
to roll in.

"How could you engage in such *lashon harah* (shit-
talking)?" yelled one particularly irate reader on my

voice mail. "I can tell by your last name that you must be Israeli. If so, even more shame on your self-hating soul."

Dealing with impassioned responses comes with the territory in the publishing industry. But this particular outburst proved illuminating for me. The beautifully crafted article that inspired such rage—written by former *Time* Jerusalem bureau chief and erstwhile crime novelist Matt Rees for our September/October 2005 edition—steered well clear of the usual hot-button topics of Israel coverage. Rees's piece examined the failure of Israel's public health care system to properly look after the country's mentally ill Holocaust survivors. It was one of those rare gems that every editor who's serious about social justice dreams of acquiring. *Tikkun* published it nearly two years before Prime Minister Ehud Olmert found himself besieged by elderly Israeli survivors in concentration camp uniforms protesting his government's offer of an estimated twenty-dollar-per-month stipend in exchange for keeping their plight out of circulation in the United States.

Yet the article elicited a reaction that I was familiar with from our coverage of the Israeli-Palestinian conflict, but had mistakenly believed would be less intense in this case. As I can now see more clearly, the caller was so incensed because he believed that both the British journalist who wrote the damaging exposé and *Tikkun* itself were questioning Israel's very right to exist. From his perspective, we were disguising our anti-Zionism by commissioning negative social coverage of Israel.

The editor in me was tempted to chalk up this reading of Rees's article to the legacy of ill will among con-

servative Jews that *Tikkun* had accumulated in the nearly
twenty years prior to my hiring. But as an Israeli I recognized that the lessons of this interaction extended much
further. My experiences at the magazine up to that point
should have clued me in that many of our readers ap-
proached our content with suspicion and even hostility.
In a sense, they expected to have their buttons pushed,
and not just by stories about the West Bank. Incidents
like this taught me that a significant portion of American Jewry didn't want to hear about Israel's failings,
period. Because the article so obviously dealt with the
ineptitude—or, as some would argue, the callousness—of
the Israeli state in caring for its most vulnerable citizens
(indeed, precisely those for whom the state was rhetori-
cally created), it struck the same chord as would have
a feature on a "break-their-bones" anti-demonstration
policy or artillery strikes on refugee camps in Lebanon.

This was the editorial conundrum I repeatedly confronted throughout my tenure at *Tikkun*. How could I, as
an Israeli citizen, take American Jews seriously if they
cared so deeply about Israel's existence, yet so little
about its actual functioning? Had their desire to discredit Arab and Palestinian claims to the country im-
paired their ability to empathize with other Jews? Or
was there a magic narrative formula that would let me
capture the plight of Israelis while working around the
paranoid stance that any discussion of Israeli social justice issues was anti-Zionist code?

I find myself confronting this problem constantly as
I try to balance my present life in the Diaspora with my
past as a person who had no choice but to identify with
Israel. It seems that I'm being displaced from the Israel

I know and, yes, love—the way you love your family despite all the things it has done to mess you up—by the Israel of American imaginings. This is an uncomfortable acknowledgment because I recognize all too well that my sense of "occupation" is a metaphor that's incommensurable with the deprivations experienced by the Palestinians for whom the meaning of that term is a matter of flesh and blood. But I've learned that it's better to be attentive to my conflicted feelings than to ignore them. I've had the privilege of living most of my adult life in the relative freedom of the affluent and liberal city of San Francisco. If I feel bound by American fantasies of Israel, how must those Israelis feel who live elsewhere in places less amenable to a diversity of perspectives?

In a sense, Israel's punishment for failing to live up to the idealized notions held by American Jews is to be imaginatively conquered by them, suffering a peculiar form of imperialism that overlooks the land's "natives"— whatever their religion or ethnicity—in much the same way that the original Zionist immigrants to Ottoman Palestine regarded their new home as a wild and empty place. Paradoxically, contemporary political discourse about Israel in the United States—even as it hinges on the opposition between Jews and Muslims, Israelis and Palestinians—ends up collapsing the very distinctions it seeks to sustain in its preference for the figure of Israel over the reality of Israel.

ISRAEL IS EVERYWHERE

In theory, a population as worldly and educated as most Jewish Americans should understand the predicament that Israelis find themselves in, since the U.S. itself suffers under the burden of stereotypes. The years since 9/11 have made painfully clear that people in other parts of the world have a difficult time distinguishing between fantasy and reality where Americans are concerned. Given the United States' imperial ambitions and un-questioned military superiority in recent decades, this misperception can't easily be transmuted into a feeling of being "occupied." But Americans who venture abroad commonly experience the sensation of only being seen for what they're expected to be, rather than for who they are as individuals. Why then is it so hard for even the most sophisticated participants in American politi-cal discourse about Israel to see through the figure of the country to the reality concealed beneath it?

The answer lies in the nature of the Diaspora's com-plex political identity. Since the founding of the Israeli state in 1948, all Jews have been considered its citizens, no matter where they live or what they believe. The ex-tension of this right has consistently strengthened Israel economically and socially over the years and prevented Jews from being hopelessly outnumbered by the Arab population still living within the nation's borders. But it has also given Jews who have no intention of ever living in Israel a political stake in the nation's affairs. As critics of the U.S. government's support for Israel have stressed for decades, this psychological investment from the Di-aspora Jewish community has translated seamlessly into a financial investment. But those critics often fail to see the degree that this support—which initially came with relatively few strings attached—has recently been accompanied by a growing desire for a specific kind of influence. Whether conscious of this desire or not, members of the Diaspora have increasingly shown that they want more for their time and money than the mere satisfaction of knowing that Israel continues to exist.

The most striking aspect of debates like l'affaire Judt is the way they underscore the collapse of traditional distinctions between Israel and the Diaspora. Already prevalent on the Jewish Right, this confusion of boundaries has spread in the wake of 9/11 to the Left as well. The significance of automatic Israeli citizenship, and the ways in which Jews experience this "birthright" (to invoke the name of the increasingly derided Zionist educational program), have been changed to such an extent that news in Israel at times ceases to be classified as "foreign affairs." Because non-Israeli Jews are encouraged to feel involved in Israel's life, some tend to assume they can participate in its politics the way they do in their own home countries, whether that be Germany, the United Kingdom, Australia, or the United States. Instead of this attachment compelling them to immigrate to Israel, many members of the Diaspora are content to participate in the nation's politics from abroad.

For members of the foreign Jewish Left, this sense of citizenship neatly parallels the strong identification with the Israeli state among conservatives in the Diaspora. In place of veneration for Jerusalem, the holy places, and the Jewish character of the Israeli state, we find on the Left a similar attachment to Israeli media and culture, and the high level of public debate that takes place in Israeli society over issues involving religion, gender, citizenship, and economics. And while both of these Israels are more figurative than literal, the material consequences of this psychic involvement are profound.

Take, for example, what many on the Right have chosen to champion as the paradigmatic instance of progressive positions on Israel: "Left anti-Semitism." Though
its promotion by conservatives is motivated in part by
a desire to discredit peace advocacy, the phenomenon
itself is entirely real. Attributed to progressives sympa-
thetic to Islamist and nationalist Arab criticisms of Israel
and Zionism, this genre of anti-Semitism is the least understood form of prejudice against Jewry. When viewed
as opportunist in its support of Islamic and right-wing
Arab views of Jews and Zionism, as a means of disguising racism as anticolonialism, left-wing anti-Semites
can almost be considered false progressives who don the
multicultural mantle of the Left in order to be openly
prejudiced.

Jews are incited against not because they practice
an inferior culture or religion, but because a key object of their faith is a state that discriminates against
non-Jews—specifically, Muslims. Since the concept of
the state is so integral to their religious identity, Jews
are seen as being inherently biased against non-Jews.
The foundational importance of the Zionist state, as an
exclusively Jewish state, is often viewed by such progressives as an iconographic instance of the core politics
of Jewish identity.

In short, Judaism is a synonym for racism because
behind it hides Israel. Progressives aren't supposed to
like Judaism for two principle reasons: first, because
Israel stands for the indivisibility of religion and state;
and second, due to Israel's official practice of discrimination against Palestinians on the basis of their ethnicity. Though Judaism is found by many progressives to be

deeply problematic, both historically and theologically, the notion of returning to a promised land is less troubling than how this is understood to function as a cover for the theft of Arab lands.

In addition to collapsing the distinction between Judaism and the Israeli state, this perspective can oftentimes appear so totalizing that it denies the possibility that there might be other ways to be politically Jewish—even if Jews acknowledge the imbrication of nationalism and religion in their spirituality. Indeed, it is an unsophisticated and at times vulgar critique of Judaism that harkens back to the most primitive Marxist critiques of religion. Unfortunately, this is not the version of progressive anti-Semitism taken to task by Jewish conservatives like Alvin Rosenthal. Yet it is one of the more impoverished, but real, consequences of the global Left's anger at Israel.

ADOPTING PALESTINE

When it was primarily the Right that identified with Israel politically, debates like l'affaire Judt were both less frequent and less intense. Although progressives began to grow increasingly skeptical of Israel in the wake of the Six-Day War, they did so under the banner of a self-conscious internationalism, so their criticism seemed abstract. The cause of the Palestinians was packed together with so many other causes in the portmanteau of the Left that it became diffuse, one instance of a worldwide problem.

As those other causes—including the peace movement, the antinuclear movement, and the women's movement—began to lose focus, attention on Israel increased, particularly following its invasion of Lebanon in June 1982. But it wasn't until the tumultuous period that followed the end of the Cold War that Israel's treatment of the Palestinians became one of the chief preoccupations of the American Left.

Even as the first intifada (1987–1991) began to decrease in intensity, its impact in the United States started to be felt more strongly. No longer having to worry so deeply about the prospect of mutually assured destruction, news-minded Americans found themselves with more time to reflect on smaller-scale conflicts around the world. The eruption of civil wars in the former Yugoslavia reminded people in the developed world how easily the veneer of civilization can wear off in the face of historically grounded ethnic antagonisms. At the same time, the tide was turning in South Africa, as the international effort in the '80s to overturn apartheid at last seemed to be having the desired effect. Finally, the first Gulf War, waged by a multinational coalition led by the United States, brought a wide range of unfinished business in the Middle East back into the headlines.

While perhaps not a perfect storm for Israel's political establishment, these developments overlapped in the media in a way that let potential critics connect the dots about the deeper implications of Israeli government policies, which even the good news of the 1993 Oslo Accords did little to alter. All of a sudden, in every televised image of a Palestinian teenager wielding a slingshot against an Israeli tank, many progressives took the opportunity not only to conclude that Israel was now Goliath to the Palestinian David, but also to elevate that realization into a principal political concern. Instead of continuing to be seen as a special case of widespread global problems, Israel now found itself in the bull's-eye of an American Left that had historically neglected the Middle East.

Israel's occupation of Lebanon, the West Bank, and Gaza provided an ideal point of entry for an ideological stance on the region in a way that the crude economism of the petropolitics associated with the Gulf War—*No Blood for Oil*—had not. By acting the part of a confident imperial force at a time when the former Soviet empire was disintegrating and the United States was unsure of its role as the sole remaining superpower, Israel helped the Left to maintain its intellectual focus. The overlapping of religion and racism in the actions of a state unapologetically committed to the project of colonization permitted the redeployment of traditional forms of political critique, imparting a desperately needed sense of continuity amid a world transformed by unexpected ruptures. In other words, focusing on Israel became the means of demonstrating that the principle ideological concerns of the Left prior to 1989 were as valid as ever.

INTRODUCING THE MIDDLE EAST

We can more fully understand recent debates about Israel within the Diaspora when we keep the immediate post–Cold War era in mind. Although technically still recent history, the 1990s are difficult for someone living in the post–9/11 era to comprehend as anything other than the "before" to our "after." The global political landscape changed so radically in the first years of the new millennium that it seems as though the previous decade got locked in a time capsule to be exhumed in a future where people will find it easier to identify broader trends. Yet we need to examine that period closely if we're serious about grasping how Israel has changed.

For one thing, the allegations that Alvin Rosenfeld and others have made about "Jewish anti-Semitism" depend upon the existence of organizations on the Left that either date from the 1990s or were formed by individuals active in campaigns against the Israeli government at that time. Although rising resistance to the Bush administration agenda, particularly the war in Iraq, sharpened progressive critiques of its Israeli allies, the foundation for them was laid before 9/11. It's true that organizations like J Street, Brit Tzedek v'Shalom, Americans for Peace Now, Israel Policy Forum, and Jewish Voice for Peace take into account how radically the American presence in the Middle East has expanded since the war in Afghanistan. But they're principally concerned with long-standing matters of Israeli government policy over which the United States, despite its support, has limited influence.

September 11 had considerably less impact on Israelis than it did on Americans. While Israel has worked more closely with the U.S. military since the attacks, the problems it faces both within and beyond its borders haven't changed a great deal since Americans woke up that day to a new world order. While America regarded 9/11 as a "day that will live in infamy," many in Israel saw it as confirmation that the reality of everyday life—where constant vigilance has long been the price of freedom—had been successfully exported to its benefactor. This isn't to imply that all Israelis were overcome with schadenfreude after the attacks on the World Trade Center and Pentagon, even though certain Israeli politicians, such as current Prime Minister Benjamin Netanyahu, have repeatedly stated that the attacks were of value to Israel.

The intensity of debates like l'affaire Judt within the Diaspora derives less from changes in Israel or the peace movement than from the decidedly subjective perception, emerging from the foreign policy of the Bush administration and its staunchest allies in the United Kingdom and Australia, that threats must be handled differently than they were in the '90s. Just as the onset of the Cold War led to changes in how America treated its Left—with the grudging tolerance of the 1930s replaced by the frenzy of McCarthyism—9/11 gave both conservatives and more mainstream Jewish leaders a reason to pay attention to the Jewish progressives like Judt, and the "loony Left," that they'd previously dismissed as being unworthy of engagement.

GOING NATIVE, ABROAD

These discussions in the Diaspora are so confusing in large part because they occur within that imaginary Israel in which both conservative and progressive Jews are so invested. The failure of both the Right and the Left in the Diaspora to see Israel as it actually is constitutes a subtle but pernicious form of intellectual imperialism. To the degree that American Jews perceive Israel as both extant at the pleasure of the U.S. government and dependent on its support (a conclusion belied, as I'll argue later, by Israel's complex relationship with Europe), they convince themselves that their position on Israeli policies must be heeded, even when that position is hopelessly colored by fantasy.

This self-delusion is even more of a problem on the

Left than the Right. Whereas conservatives of the post–9/11 era have generally advanced an ideological agenda that champions idealism over realpolitik (there's no other way to understand the Bush administration's Middle East policy short of degenerating into conspiracy theory), progressives tend to believe they can see facts that others overlook. Noam Chomsky, a secular American Jew and one of the most prominent critics of the Israeli government's treatment of Palestinians since the Six-Day War, is a prime example. Chomsky consistently points out how the ruling powers in both the U.S. and Israel hide the truth about what has really transpired since the occupation of the territories in 1967. Although younger peace activists may not agree with Chomsky on many points (and may resent the way his stature draws attention from their efforts), they generally agree that they're fighting a struggle for revelation. The trouble is that they're actually maneuvering within a political field in which too much is already in plain view.

This confidence in the power of truth telling reflects a positive conception of Israel that circulates within the Diaspora Left. Whereas conservatives love the coupling of religion and power embodied in the Israeli state, progressives often fetishize the Israeli public sphere, and they contrast the intensity and openness of the debates it fosters with the "censorship by the bottom line" that's come to prevail in the United States.

While conservatives generally regard this tendency on the Left as another way in which anti-Zionist Jews seek to undermine Israel, they'd do well to consider the matter more carefully. As critical as progressives may be of Israeli government policies, they share with their con-

servative counterparts an investment in the continuation of
the political reality that makes such debates possible; progressives sense that the very presence of open discourse is
inextricably bound up with the positive aspects of Israeli
society, and wish to see those elements constitute a more
inclusive, truly multiethnic Israeli democracy.

WHEN THE LEFT BANK REPLACED THE WEST BANK

Israel's tradition of self-criticism—by its liberal civil
servants and left-wing activists, and by specific internationally distributed representatives of its media—has
become a shining beacon of political virtue to many non-
Israeli Jewish liberals. In a sense, these critics embody
the political and moral conscience that the Israeli government and its foreign policy seem to have lost in the
years following the Six-Day War. While valuing these
aspects of Israeli life ultimately mirrors in some respects
the conservative fetishization of Israel in the Diaspora,
there's still something redemptive about this strange
coinvestment in the Jewish state, even if it's based in
a preference for the figure of Israel over the reality of
Israel.

As confused as the Diaspora Left may appear, its vision of reforming Israel as a state is real. The Left retains
an admirably optimistic desire to correct Israel's deficits
in accordance with the standards of a European-style,
multicultural social democracy. Diaspora Jews may not
agree completely on whether a one- or two-state deal
solves the Palestinian-Israeli conflict, or whether a
market-based or government-dominated public sector
can adequately redress the country's high levels of social inequality. But they all seem to assume that reform

can indeed be created within—or perhaps despite—Israel's highly overdetermined and confining historical context.

When the Jewish Right goes after people like Tony Judt or the less provocative peace organizations on the Left, it risks ruining the remaining basis for solidarity within the Diaspora—the belief that a better Israel can be made from the current one. That's not to imply that the Right's fears are groundless. The emergence of a new Jewish Left in the Diaspora warrants some of the sensational rhetoric meted out by conservatives in media and academic environments. When taken to their logical conclusion, the political concerns of progressives do indeed contradict every defining feature of the Israeli status quo: religious traditionalism, racism, social inequality, and colonialism. That's why, as *Occupied Minds* author Arthur Neslen explained in a January 2007 interview in *Tikkun*, ending Israel's occupation of its remaining Palestinian territorial assets is a much bigger deal than simply withdrawing from the land itself.

Advocating withdrawal from the Occupied Territories calls into question the character of the modern Israeli state and everything that comes along with it. You don't change your character simply by taking a few steps backward. But it is crucial to remember that those features of the status quo, which have become more prominent in the four decades since the Six-Day War, are still not set in stone. The reality of contemporary Israel is more complex than that. And, while there is ample ground for despair, there's also reason to hope. So much of the increasing polarization of debate is generational. Change is coming, no matter how fiercely some resist it.

The question is whether this change is able to success-fully manifest itself in an Israeli context.

LOOKING OVER THE WALL

Right after Christmas in 2007, I received a call from my friend Charlie, who noted the number of times he had heard references to checkpoints in coverage of the holi-day observances in Bethlehem. He observed how well integrated these references were with the usual holiday reporting, as though they were as natural as the imagery we associate with celebrating Christmas in the birth-place of Jesus: pilgrims praying, lights illuminating the ancient interior of the Church of Nativity, the local chil-dren eagerly joining the religious procession, and so on.

Despite attempts by the Diaspora press to be up-beat about Israel in the weeks immediately following the November 2007 conference in Annapolis, its holiday celebration coverage in the West Bank revealed some wariness—not just by the European news outlets like the BBC that Jewish conservatives find so biased, but by certain branches of the American press as well.

A Christmas Eve NPR *Morning Edition* story on foreign graffiti artists decorating the Bethlehem portion of the separation wall epitomized Charlie's observation. Not only did the piece focus on the holiday timing of their event, but its discussion of the ingenious work of the graffiti artists assembled—specifically that of British icon Banksy and the lesser known Spanish artist SAM3 (named after a Cold War–era Russian antiaircraft missile)—made it impossible to overlook the political implications of their art. Discussing murals that made comical yet pointed ref-erence to local power relationships—little girls patting down Israeli soldiers, troops checking the IDs of donkeys, etc.—the report suggested that Westerners might have acquired the capacity to see the town as a place under occupation and suffering from Israeli-imposed deprivation rather than as a storybook city mismanaged by its stereotypically uncivilized native inhabitants. While the human capacity to fetishize should never be underestimated—this revisionist portrait of Bethlehem could surely inspire listeners to fantasize about touring an "authentic" Holy Land—the increasing frequency of this kind of reporting must be considered a salutary development.

Although the segment covered a cultural event in the contested West Bank, it highlighted how the values that the Diaspora instinctively attaches to Israel are slowly but surely changing. Artists travel from Europe to Bethlehem to criticize Israeli colonialism, and American radio journalists cover it for mainstream news outlets for prime time playback during the holiday season. This is the new status quo. To return to Judt's point, even if the situation in Bethlehem itself changed little, the view of it within the U.S. had changed plenty.

This helps to explain why even mainstream American coverage of Israel's incursion into Gaza the following December steered clear of the demonization of the Arab world that had once been de rigueur. Although the more hidebound members of the progressive community continued to rehash the familiar arguments about media bias, their numbers seemed to be dwindling. Instead of crying "Censorship!" the Left increasingly turned to establishment news sources to ground its critique of Israel's reaction to the provocations of Hamas.

Links posted on social networking sites like Facebook exemplified this trend. While do-it-yourself reports by citizen journalists and documentary footage distributed by Arab networks operating out of Gaza played an important role in the Left's response to the Israeli offensive in December 2008, so did, however grudgingly, CNN— and, as a number of pundits pointed out, a noticeably agitated *New York Times*. It's now apparent that l'affaire Judt had foreshadowed a more comprehensive change in the way Israel is represented in the United States.

We've yet to see how much the Diaspora's growing familiarity with the Middle East might help to demythologize the region in a way that renders this type of coverage less controversial. Though conservatives will continue to ascribe such reportage to anti-Jewish bias, they're really objecting to the West simply accumulating local knowledge about the fabled region. This increased awareness is bound to inspire disillusionment—both in the literal sense of being disappointed with Israel, and in Max Weber's sociological sense in which power seems no longer "enchanted" or beyond reach. Perhaps that's the push American Jews need to realize that there are better ways of spending their time and money than waging war within the *New York Review of Books*.

CHAPTER THREE

THE TERMS OF ISRAEL CRITICISM

National Public Radio's 2007 coverage of the Christmas celebration in the Holy Land exemplified what many conservatives regard as a disturbing trend in American coverage of Israel. By focusing attention on the struggle of Palestinians whose livelihoods depend more on tourism to Bethlehem than on the celebration itself, the feature was a potent reminder that the mainstream media is increasingly willing to confer legitimacy on perspectives that had previously been excluded from view. Should the Right in both Israel and the Diaspora extend the suspicions that have long been directed toward the BBC and other Western European media organizations—which they see as enablers of terrorism for presenting an Arab point of view—to their American counterparts? If so, wouldn't that suggest a dangerous increase in Israel's global isolation?

For some conservatives, the answer to these questions was an unequivocal yes. But others were less certain. While generational change may have been the biggest reason for this restraint, there were other factors working to confuse the issue. Most notably, the increasing prominence of guerrilla media in conflict zones like the Middle East made it hard to determine the motivations for stories such as the NPR feature. When someone like Salam Jamal Kanaan, a Palestinian teenager, can covertly videotape an Israeli soldier shooting a handcuffed Palestinian prisoner at point-blank range, it's hard to argue that citizen journalism isn't real journalism. Especially when that footage ends up on YouTube, scoops traditional reporting on such events, and leads to an official inquiry after an alleged cover-up of the incident by the Israeli armed forces. In other words, the trend toward legitimizing a wider range of perspectives might have more to do with bigger structural changes in the media than in the political arena they report. Coverage has become much broader and more variegated than was the case in the era of top-down television, radio, and newspaper reporting, even if it frequently lacks the depth, continuity, and tight direction of that period.

Due to this proliferation of media perspectives, we no longer know where we're supposed to stand or with whose vision we're supposed to identify. On the contrary, if we align ourselves with anything, it is often with an increasingly flexible media apparatus that makes it possible for us to disidentify. The remarkable number of individuals reporting on the same events, insisting that every story be triangulated through multiple sources, now reflects the objectivity that traditional journalism once aspired toward. Not that we've reached the point where we give all perspectives equal credence—money and power still talk. But there's also never been a time like this, in which private individuals operating on tiny budgets can communicate their content in ways that make it impossible to deny there are problems with Israel's treatment of the Palestinians that cannot be explained away as a product of anti-Semitism, media bias, or anti-Zionist ideology.

People around the world have been learning this lesson (sometimes the hard way) with the explosive growth in user-generated content. Perhaps it just took a little longer for supporters of Israel in the Diaspora, whose paranoid visions—however justified from the standpoint of history—tend to limit their powers of perception. Still, the fact that they have begun to use the same social media tools to generate counterpropaganda—rewriting Wikipedia pages on Israel to represent the "Israeli" point of view, and even justifying the surprise attack on Gaza through popular applications such as Twitter—has done little to transform global opinion. The content, after all, is still the problem. And, if anything, the rapid growth in alternative means of delivering content only reinforces the breadth of the problem. Even if it's the same story, seeing it framed in dozens of different ways, from YouTube to France 24 to Flickr, magnifies the perception that it matters.

MANAGING THE EUROPEAN LEFT

Most traditional newspapers have gone through major changes as the era of new media has led to the gradual erosion of subscription bases and advertising revenue. But it's different for periodicals like the English online edition of Israeli newspaper *Ha'aretz*, which is published in a small country with a densely packed public sphere. New media does level the playing field, not just for amateur wildcat reporters with a blog or camcorder, but also for established publications that come from geographic, economic, and ideological positions that were marginalized during the heyday of twentieth-century media conglomerates. The ninety-one-year-old Middle Eastern publication now has both the exciting potential and wearying burden of mattering to an international audience that resists easy categorization.

Instead of taking its traditional readership's politics for granted—patriotic but highly critical of the Israeli Right—the paper must now convey its positions to readers who have far less in common with its writers. Indeed, *Ha'aretz*'s ability to both articulate classically Jewish concerns and exhibit a political orientation that at times echoes historical materialism can bewilder anyone not schooled in the history of Zionism. Outside of Israel, where such historical ignorance prevails even among the country's strong supporters, the confusion about the newspaper's politics, and what it says about Israeli politics, is magnified.

Indiana University scholar Alvin Rosenfeld's assertion that Jewish critics of Israel are functionally anti-Semitic seemed to hit a nerve even with some left-leaning Israelis. *Ha'aretz* avoided taking a stand during three months of open intellectual warfare in the Diaspora, but finally printed an official statement on what constitutes legitimate criticism of the government's practices.

Unambiguously titled "Israel's Existence Is Not a Question," the March 2007 editorial was both an exercise in Israeli self-criticism and an admonition to Diaspora leftists to dispense with critiques that challenge the country's right to sovereignty. The editorial opens with an anecdote in which German Chancellor Angela Merkel told the 2007 European-Israeli Dialogue conference that she was sorry that she had to repeatedly remind people that "defending Israel's right to exist will continue to stand at the center of German foreign policy." As welcome as Merkel's remarkably frank statement is, it indicates how much Israel's legitimacy as a nation-state has eroded.

According to the editors of *Ha'aretz*, a reactionary minority that doesn't represent the true political views of most Israelis engineered this crisis. Since the 1967 war, *Ha'aretz* argues, this minority has "assumed a belligerent monopoly on the Land of Israel and on Jewish identity" that replaced the liberal Zionism of Theodor Herzl "with a messianic, separatist, antihumanistic Judaism of muscle." This group—presumably the constellation of settlers, security conservatives, and religious nationalists who have long antagonized the country's progressives—effectively seized control of the Israeli state and forced the country to forget its founding purpose: to create a national home for Jews "with equal rights and obligations in the family of modern nations." Instead, they traded this goal for a national identity founded on a Holocaust-born concept of victimization that has fostered Israeli distrust of an outside world that will inevitably reject them. As a result, when European leftists and their American counterparts criticize Israel, they depict the country as an ethno-religious enterprise that by virtue of its anachronistic nationalist character is guaranteed a short life. *Ha'aretz* sees this as anti-Jewish racism masquerading as progressive politics that seeks to replace a colonial regime with its indigenous Palestinian other.

The editorial concludes by offering its own liberal alternative: "Israel's policies are worthy of severe con-

demnation," it states, "but its right to exist is absolute."
Ha'aretz's desire to stake out such an ideological middle
ground contrasts starkly with the Manichean discursive
orthodoxy promoted by Jewish American Zionists like
Alvin Rosenfeld. Instead of implying that all external
criticism of Israel is ultimately aimed at destroying the
nation and its inhabitants, the *Ha'aretz* editorial reaches
a more moderate conclusion: one may criticize Israeli
politics and government policy, but not the Jewish right
to statehood. Whereas Rosenfeld argues that criticizing
Israel is itself anti-Semitic, *Ha'aretz* uncovers racism in a
specific kind of leftist orientation toward Israeli foreign
policy.

What the *Ha'aretz* analysis shares with Rosenfeld's
essay on anti-Semitism is a concern with the way that
the Diaspora Left thinks about Israel. Although many
examples of leftist anti-Zionism match its criteria—U.S.
foreign policy critic Jeffrey Blankfort, for example, or
the British Respect Party MP George Galloway—the
Ha'aretz piece unfortunately chooses to use the British
newspaper the *Guardian* as its primary straw man. Referring to an editorial that the newspaper supposedly
ran in 2004 as an example of European leftists' "efforts
to undermine, on principle, [Israel's] right to exist as a
Jewish state," *Ha'aretz* makes a deeply revealing factual
error. It cites the *Guardian* editorial's title as "Does Israel
Have a Right to Exist?"—but the British periodical never
ran a piece with that title. What it did run was a much
tougher-named opinion editorial by a Muslim journalist
in January 2001, not in 2004.

Entitled "Israel Simply Has No Right to Exist," this
controversial op-ed, written by the then relatively un-

known pundit Faisal Bodi, argues that Jews have no right to national sovereignty because their claim to Israel is based on religious rather than rational sources:

> Certainly there is no moral case for the existence of Israel. Israel stands as the realisation of a biblical statement. Former Prime Minister Golda Meir famously delineated its raison d'être. "This country exists as the accomplishment of a promise made by God Himself. It would be absurd to call its legitimacy into account."
>
> That biblical promise is Israel's only claim to legitimacy. But whatever God meant when he promised Abraham that "unto thy seed have I given this land, from the river of Egypt unto the great river, the Euphrates," it is doubtful that he intended it to be used as an excuse to take by force and chicanery a land lawfully inhabited and owned by others.

On the surface, this is simply a secular refutation of the most superficial religious argument on behalf of the Jewish right to return to the Promised Land: Bodi is asking why Jews believe something so deeply that's only justified by a myth. But this is significant because plenty of left-wing Zionists might actually reject this religious rationale for national legitimacy. When the Jewish right to land is rationalized as being divinely ordained, opponents of the settlements in territory that doesn't technically belong to Israel have every reason to be wary. From the *Ha'aretz* perspective, however, the misattributed *Guardian* piece makes the mistake of responding to Israel's dispossession of the Palestinians not by attacking Israeli political policy, but by employing a leftist critique of religion to undermine the country's right to exist.

The world is full of Faisal Bodis, not to mention a wealth of far less reasonable people who want to see Israel wiped from the map. But that's hardly a new development. The *Ha'aretz* editorial ably demonstrates the fear that Bodi's arguments will be legitimized by the Left in places like the United Kingdom, just as the PLO had been in the 1970s. Its authors perceive such arguments as a renewed threat to Israel's existence posed by progressives who identify with the Palestinian cause, a threat that they ironically facilitate by identifying Bodi's piece with the *Guardian* itself—an uncharacteristically paranoid move by *Ha'aretz*.

Aside from getting their facts wrong, the *Ha'aretz* editorial's authors also overlooked how the British newspaper has also published the work of many liberal Zionist authors, such as Israeli novelist David Grossman. Yet even if the *Ha'aretz* editorial is guilty of a deeply problematic error, it must be understood that the way that Israel is constructed in the Diaspora guarantees larger-than-life responses from both its supporters and its detractors. The editorial demonstrates how even Israeli progressives often see the need to exaggerate as a response to the extreme positions between which they must navigate. Because the middle ground is so hotly contested where Israel is concerned, those caught in the crossfire between radical positions feel like they must shout to be heard.

THERE'S ALWAYS SEX

The image of Israel as the "United States of the Middle East," proof that democracy and modernity can flourish in a region portrayed by Western conservatives as the antithesis of civilization, is becoming increasingly hard to find. The dissenting view suggests instead that Israel's achievements are dubious, serving primarily to confirm its status as an outsider to peaceful global affairs. Israel is an ethnocracy, where the government routinely violates international law in its quest to extend Jewish dominance on the basis of religious claims. From a military perspective, Israeli behavior is equally transgressive of liberal norms. Israel's armed forces are consistently blamed for not distinguishing between combatants and civilians, and are condemned for committing acts of ethnic cleansing and war crimes. Often the subject of failed boycott initiatives and divestment campaigns, Israel is perceived by an increasing number of westerners as a racist police state in the tradition of apartheid-era South Africa.

Despite the Israeli government's best attempts to portray itself as a modern Western country that embodies all of the same liberal political and cultural values as Europe and the U.S., those efforts frequently backfire. Decades of poor PR culminated in very negative coverage of Israel during the second Lebanon war and then during its three-week campaign in Gaza between December 2008 and January 2009; despite banning journalists from reporting within the territory, the outside world still managed to witness the immense collateral damage inflicted by Israeli forces.

Significantly, though the latter operation was better coordinated from a military perspective and appeared, at least initially, to have been a tactical success, it also demonstrated that Israel had failed to make similar gains on the PR front. Although Israel's Foreign Ministry had initiated a number of campaigns in the months following the Lebanon conflict to correct the damage it had caused to the country's reputation (including hiring a New York–based advertising firm to "rebrand" the country), it only made matters worse.

In 2007, Israeli Foreign Ministry officials were publicly accused of seeking to curb the growing coverage of Israeli citizens critical of the occupation. In France, the Israeli Embassy reportedly threatened to withdraw its sponsorship of a local Jewish film festival because it was hosting *Forgiveness*, a film by Israeli director Udi Aloni. The movie tells the story of an Jewish American volunteer to the Israel Defense Forces who suffers a nervous breakdown after he kills a Palestinian girl, and is subsequently committed to a mental institution. That narrative is unsettling enough from a PR perspective. But because the mental institution also happens to be built on the ruins of a Palestinian village destroyed by Israeli forces in 1948, the film's allegorical implications are even more disturbing.

That same winter, the Israeli consulate in Los Angeles put out an all-points bulletin to American consular offices advising them to keep an eye on a select group of Israelis lecturing around the U.S. about the occupation. They were members of Breaking the Silence, an organization of IDF and Fatah veterans traveling the country together to demonstrate the ability to collaborate across national lines. Los Angeles Consul General Ehud Danoch made headlines when it emerged that he had excoriated U.S. Jewish peace organization Brit Tzedek v'Shalom for sponsoring the Breaking the Silence tour in an official report to the Foreign Ministry in Jerusalem—thereby revealing that the Israeli government had been tracking the group's activities. Danoch made it clear that his Israeli government offices were attempting to curtail not only the rights of Israeli citizens to speak freely about their country's foreign policy, but also those of American Jews.

The Israeli government's PR attempts took another hit when a story in June of 2007 revealed that the country's consulate in New York had successfully proposed that the men's magazine *Maxim* put together a semi-pornographic spread of former female soldiers called "Women of the IDF." A source connected to the consulate explained that the project was intended to help reverse the declining interest in Israel among Jewish men between the ages of eighteen and thirty-five. The feature itself boasted some fairly symptomatic quotes from many of the women profiled, including one named Yarden who waxed provocatively about how much she likes firing her M-16.

First broken in the Diaspora by the *Guardian*, the story quotes Israeli parliamentarians Zahava Gal-On (Meretz) and Colette Avital (Labor) condemning the consulate for taking such action. "It is unfortunate that the New York consulate thinks that Israel's relevance will be expressed by the use of naked women who are treated as an object, and not as women of substance who exude achievement and success," Gal-On stated. Avital asserted that the *Maxim* article was a "pornographic campaign to encourage tourism." Providing his own analysis of the consulate's dubious move, former *Guardian* correspondent Conal Urquhart notes: "Israel is keen to sell itself as a Western country with beaches and nightclubs rather than a country full of religious zealots which has been in a permanent state of emergency since its creation."

Regardless of what Israeli officials might have been trying to metaphorically conceal, these efforts contained an element of cynicism that cannot be ignored. For one thing, they reflect a poor view of Diaspora Jews, as unsophisticated, easily susceptible to such base forms of nationalist propaganda. This was an attempt to reassert the original libidinal connection between Diaspora Jewry and their motherland, with all of the gendered baggage that logically accompanies this appeal to such a clichéd Oedipal reflex. For another, it also communicates an illuminating conception of what media ought to do for Israel abroad. The only way to disguise all of the pain and conflict that the *Guardian* reports—which forces *Ha'aretz* to ask its liberal readers to not question Israel's basic right to exist—is to, quite literally, turn to pornography.

ACKNOWLEDGING DIVERSITY

These incidents underscore how difficult it is to steer the publicity Israel receives in a positive direction. Suppression of oppositional voices from Israel or the Diaspora won't change the country's unfavorable perception in the world; nor will a fashion spread of sexy former soldiers, for that matter. Each of these examples suggests that there's something seriously wrong with both the national image that Israeli government officials want to project and their strategies for changing hearts and minds abroad. The widening gulf between the two conceptions of Israel that dominate global discourse becomes painfully apparent in these ill-conceived attempts to the sell the country to an international audience that isn't buying.

Whatever the reality of actually existing Israel—a devilishly elusive entity—its custodians appear to think that the best way to generate love for it is through direct government intervention. While things haven't yet descended to the cynicism of May Day parades in the former Eastern bloc, one senses an unhealthy kind of nostalgia for it in such initiatives. No wonder, then, that Israeli periodicals like *Ha'aretz* seek to explicitly distinguish between criticizing the nation's governmental policies and its right to exist. The best PR isn't a tourism campaign, but evidence that Israel's public sphere still makes room for opinions that decry mistaken policy.

Fortunately, many members of the Diaspora Left have refrained from simplistically blaming all of Israel for the nation's problems. In this sense, the audience that *Ha'aretz* desires already exists. It is nurtured by the arguments of prominent Jewish American philosophers like Judith Butler, who, despite her support for divestment from Israel in the early 2000s, has argued against academic boycotts of the country. She has forcefully underscored the dangers of conflating the policies of a state with the convictions of its inhabitants. "The very possibility of significant dissent depends on recognising the difference between them," wrote Butler in her August 2003 essay, "No, It's Not Anti-Semitic," published in the *London Review of Books*.

Written in response to British academic Mona Baker's controversial decision to dismiss two Israeli scholars from the editorial board of her translation journal in protest of Israeli government actions, Butler's argument suggests that there's far more agreement across national lines than ideologues on both the Left and Right would care to admit. "It is one thing to oppose Israel in its current form and practices or, indeed, to have critical questions about Zionism itself," concludes Butler, "but it is quite another to oppose 'Jews' or assume that all 'Jews' have the same view, that they are all in favour of Israel, identified with Israel, or represented by Israel."

Butler's words may be difficult for even progressive Zionists to hear, but they signal a salutary maturation in the Diaspora Left's thinking about Israel. Plenty of leftists, like their right-wing counterparts in the Diaspora, are still in thrall to a fantasy of Israel that pushes reality to the side. But the tide seems to be slowly turning, whether for the generational reasons I've mentioned earlier or perhaps due to the influence of antiessentialist discourses like Butler's. These two possible explanations are like opposite sides of the same coin, since the fracturing of identity politics is a historical development that's been ably sped up by a theoretical vanguard. It may seem ironic that a model borrowed from Marxism provides such an apt description of the rise of a post–Cold War Left fiercely opposed to its authoritarian tendencies. But the fact remains that the multicultural worldview, particularly when combined with the teeth of a critique of international capitalism, would never have penetrated so far into the fabric of everyday life in the developed world without the assistance of intellectuals like Butler or, for that matter, their allies at publications like *Ha'aretz* and the *Guardian*.

Although I heartily applaud this significant development, it must be considered in tandem with the negative consequences of the attempt to make people disidentify with their country. Butler's argument about distinguishing between the state and its people is absolutely correct, yet it doesn't account for individuals either collapsing that divide (whether consciously or unconsciously) with their own powers of fantasy, or losing their capacity to undertake positive action as citizens. What happens when one is called upon to act in concert with people who are unwilling or unable to make such distinctions? How can strategic disidentification coexist with identifications that are tactically necessary? And what can be done to inspire the sort of passionate attachments that many of the Israeli government's dismal PR efforts have tried and failed to produce?

Just as Jews in the Diaspora have difficulty distinguishing between their ideas of Israel and the actually existing state in which (though technically able to carry its passport) they still function as foreigners, Israelis are finding it hard to perceive the limits to their nationality. In both cases, Israel's unique conception of citizenship makes matters worse. The fact that so many potential Israelis live outside the nation's territory while a sizeable percentage of its inhabitants are denied its full protections reinforces the sense that Israel is as much a state of mind as a geographic entity.

The ambiguous nature of Israeli statehood also adds to the confusion generated by the changes in the media that I mentioned at the beginning of this chapter. It's no accident that Israeli government officials are trying to micromanage the nation's PR at a time when it's increasingly difficult to control the media. Nor is it surprising that a respected paper like *Ha'aretz* can indulge an uncharacteristic tendency to go into panic mode when confronting the representation of Israel in the Diaspora. The ease with which references to Israel slip from the literal to the metaphoric derives first and foremost from the circumstances that led to the nation's founding. But it's abetted by new media's tendency to promote the metaphorization of locality at a more general level; on the Internet, it's hard to know where you are, and it's easy to imaginatively occupy spaces to which you're denied physical access. That's what *Ha'aretz*'s devoted Diaspora readers experience, and it helps explain why the newspaper has become confused about its place in the global media.

HA'ARETZ AS ISRAEL

When I worked at *Tikkun*, *Ha'aretz*'s then chief U.S. correspondent, Shmuel Rosner, was the subject of intense scrutiny by all of the journalists I knew who covered the Middle East. "How could such a progressive newspaper employ such a Neanderthal?" was a common refrain. "He must be a buffer in Washington." I remember another editor at *Tikkun* insisting that "the guy was acting on orders from Tel Aviv," which probably sounds absurd to most people who understand *Ha'aretz*'s place within the Israeli public sphere. As I was wont to reply, Rosner was simply a conservative journalist, one of several on *Ha'aretz*'s staff. Why he was appointed to his position, given *Ha'aretz*'s liberal editorial trajectory, was something that the newspaper must have had its own good reasons for doing.

Despite my desire to not get into it with my colleagues, I could appreciate their consternation. Openly expressing his admiration for President Bush's Middle East policies and Christian Zionists like Pastor John Hagee, while routinely chastising important Jewish American liberals like the New Israel Fund's Larry Garber and J Street's Jeremy Ben-Ami, Rosner seemed particularly out of place in an American context. If he was so critical of Jewish liberals, why had he been assigned the responsibility for covering such a politically diverse community in the first place? Yet because he was his periodical's main eye on the United States and was always self-consciously writing as an Israeli in America—intensely anxious about the impact of American attitudes toward Israel—you had to read him. Warts and all, Rosner's Domain, as his blog on *Ha'aretz*'s website was called, was its own daily event.

Unfortunately, Rosner achieved a new level of irritation to much of his U.S. readership during the 2008 presidential campaign. Criticizing Barack Obama's candidacy at nearly every opportunity, the journalist's discomfort with the Illinois senator was sometimes so pronounced that it made regular readers of *Ha'aretz*'s English edition ask why the periodical didn't consistently offer opposing opinions to balance things out. Many journalists I know rationalized Rosner's prominent presence in the paper as an attempt to redress its overtly liberal stance on most domestic Israeli issues. It's hard to conceive of an equivalent situation in the American print media. And the paper's near monopoly over an important segment of the Anglophone Diaspora further amplified the tension.

Indeed, until the middle of 2008, when *Ha'aretz* began running opinion editorials more favorable toward

Obama, readers seeking an enlightened take on U.S. policy toward Israel were forced to turn, ironically enough, to the *Guardian*, where they would find regular pro-Obama editorials by progressive Israelis such as former peace negotiator Daniel Levy and *Palestine-Israel Journal* editor Hillel Schenker. Sympathizing with the concerns about Obama that were being promoted by Jewish American conservatives, and consistently questioning the new president's credentials, Rosner's criticisms of the presidential candidate came across as a calculated attempt to discredit him and encourage Jewish American readers to consider the alternatives: Hillary Clinton and, after the Democratic primaries, Republican presidential nominee John McCain. While Rosner did, eventually, moderate his tone—whether out of expediency or conviction remains unclear—memories of his vitriol during the primaries were not so easily forgotten.

If Rosner's animus against the American presidential candidate hadn't coincided with other changes at *Ha'aretz*, liberals might have written it off as a disturbing but rare exception to the paper's traditional editorial stance. But when news broke right at the apex of Rosner's attacks that several progressive members of *Ha'aretz*'s staff were leaving the periodical, the conspiracy-minded wondered whether the exception might be turning into the rule. Coupled with the fact that *Ha'aretz* had also begun running an irregular blog by Israeli President Shimon Peres, this development had the paper's international readers wondering whether, after four years under the editorial leadership of David Landau, it might be responding to pressure from the Diaspora. Could the growing readership of the English-language edition have upset *Ha'aretz*'s delicate balance between its Zionist and leftist influences?

A circulated e-mail by legendary *Ha'aretz* correspondent Amira Hass did little to allay these fears. Pointing an accusatory finger at the newspaper's new editor, Dov Alfon, Hass explained with great—some would say excessive—care that contrary to many of the rumors, she had not been laid off by the paper, but was instead in the process of renegotiating her contract following an unpaid leave of absence. After stating that Israel has "democracy for Jews" in which the "right for freedom of thought, expression, and information is fairly guaranteed," she also made a point of noting that it's a country in which "there is no OBLIGATION to exercise these liberties." Hass didn't need to be more specific; what her distinction implied was evident, even if she had conveyed it with admirable restraint.

In what read like a reply to Hass, *Ha'aretz*'s new editor gave his own explanation of what was happening on the very same day. Addressed to two readers of the English edition who had written him with their concerns, the bilingual e-mail took pains to explain how progressive the newspaper remained despite the staff changes. Citing a number of recent articles that clearly "spoke truth to power," the letter went on to point out that it was the new editor himself who back in 1994 had championed one of *Ha'aretz*'s more outspoken, surviving progressive correspondents, Gideon Levy. How could Alfon be presiding over an ideological transformation of *Ha'aretz* considering his own history of commissioning and supporting such progressive work at the paper? Suggesting that these rumors might be part of a right-wing campaign, he explained that like a lot of other periodicals, the paper was struggling financially. It simply needed to trim its payroll, he concluded, and had let go of an equal number of conservatives. (Shmuel Rosner was among those dismissed, though news of his departure did not surface until later.)

Reading this correspondence in my San Francisco office, I thought of the heartfelt devotion many American Jews have to *Ha'aretz*. For some, indeed, the newspaper inspires the sort of passionate attachment to Israel that the country's government does not. In truth, *Ha'aretz* is about the only liberal Jewish periodical that speaks to their needs. Since there's so little coverage of specifically Israeli issues in the American media, this newspaper, published several thousand miles away, is sometimes the only source for such stories. Even if it struggles sometimes to capture the American political scene properly, *Ha'aretz*'s ability to distill the complexities of the Middle East for readers desperate for measured discourse ensures its continued importance in the Diaspora. The simple fact that *Ha'aretz* has been willing to invoke the word "apartheid" to describe Israel's colonial order in the West Bank testifies to an editorial courage that's all the more valuable because it is so rare amongst Jewish publications.

Should *Ha'aretz* truly change its editorial policies, as some progressives had feared, the consequences would be grave. Despite the paper's limited distribution in Israel—Tel Aviv is just about the only place one sees it regularly—its ideological influence far exceeds its newsstand sales, particularly with those who work in government. That influence, along with its international readership, testifies to the paper's immense political and social significance, and explains why readers take the political orientation of the newspaper's individual reporters so seriously.

Many Diaspora Jewish liberals fetishize the paper and fear for its future precisely because its Israel coverage frequently points the way toward a better nation to come, though one that seems further away with each passing year. As crucial as it is to have an oppositional press to remind us of such disjunctures, it is also important to remember that periodicals serving this function will always be threatened by the circumstances that distance them from power.

CHAPTER FOUR

APARTHEID AND ITS SURPLUSES

W hen former President Jimmy Carter traveled to Israel in April 2008, he might have been received as a hero in honor of his work to broker the 1979 Camp David Accords and the many peacekeeping trips he's made to trouble spots around the world since leaving office. But instead, all but a few government leaders shunned him. By writing the 2006 book *Palestine: Peace, Not Apartheid*, Carter had swapped the mantle of peace for the mantle of controversy. Now he had come to the Middle East to defy an American and Israeli boycott on meeting with Hamas and open a dialogue that might reduce tension in the region. Predictably, Israeli Prime Minister Ehud Olmert and other members of the ruling coalition decided that they would find "scheduling conflicts" rather than meet with him.

To be sure, these Israeli leaders weren't prepared to denounce Carter publicly, both out of consideration for his international reputation and, one would hope, appreciation for his past efforts to achieve peace in the Middle East. But the message was still clear enough to provoke *Ha'aretz* to publish a damning editorial. "The boycott will not be remembered as a glorious moment in this government's history," its author coolly stated, making a point of comparing Carter's wide-ranging peace efforts to the paltry achievements of the Israeli leaders responsible for his disrespectful treatment. Then they came to the punch line. Reminding readers that it was Carter's book that initially led to him becoming a persona non grata, the editorial forcefully defended his decision to use the term "apartheid" in discussing Israel's treatment of the Palestinian people:

> Israel is not ready for such comparisons, even though the situation begs it. It is doubtful whether it is possible to complain when an outside observer, especially a former U.S. president who is well versed in international affairs, sees in the system of separate roads for Jews and Arabs, the lack of freedom of movement, Israel's control over Palestinian lands and their confiscation, and especially the continued settlement activity, which contravenes all promises Israel made and signed, a matter that cannot be accepted.

This would have been a strong statement on its own. But the sentence that followed took *Ha'aretz*'s criticism of the Israeli regime to a new level: "The interim political situation in the territories has crystallized into a kind of apartheid that has been ongoing for forty years."

This wasn't just an explanation of why Carter felt justified in deploying the term "apartheid," but approval of its use. The courage demonstrated by editorials like this has made *Ha'aretz* a beacon of hope in the progressive Diaspora, despite the newspaper's frequently confusing attempts to assert its liberal Zionist credentials on the international stage. Although plenty of Israelis agree with *Ha'aretz*'s position, there are few opportunities for them to articulate their perspective in settings where meaningful solidarity is possible. Because *Ha'aretz* has mainstream legitimacy, its willingness to take controversial stands makes it a surrogate for those who lack the resources to mobilize themselves into a public force. Although such surrogacy falls short of true political change, it is a step in the right direction.

THE ANTI-BUSH

Right after interviewing Carter with my former employer Rabbi Michael Lerner for the January/February 2007 edition of *Tikkun*, I went home and rifled through a cabinet drawer, looking for the only memento of his administration that my wife and I own. Our home is full of vintage political kitsch from all over the world, but, for all of his virtues, Jimmy Carter doesn't hold a candle to John F. Kennedy, Richard Nixon, or Ronald Reagan in the memorabilia department. The item I looked for wasn't American, but Israeli: it was a commemorative phone card from Israel's state telecommunications company, Bezeq, featuring a picture of Jimmy Carter flanked by the late Egyptian President Anwar Sadat and Israeli Prime Minister Menachem Begin.

I had held onto the card after I spent it, thinking that it would develop some kind of surplus worth at a later date. But this was hardly what I had in mind. If you'd asked me in previous decades which American politician was least likely to be demonized by Jewish hard-liners in Israel and the Diaspora alike, I would have responded "Jimmy Carter" without hesitation. Once too boring to bother wasting my home's precious display space on, Carter now needed to be out where everyone could see him.

Palestine: Peace, Not Apartheid was on everyone's mind in the Diaspora. Even people whom I had heard make arguments similar to Carter's in the past were uneasy that he'd seemingly chosen sides against their second homeland. Although most were careful to accord him the respect that Israel's leaders had refused during the former president's April 2008 visit to Israel, I still detected a sense of betrayal in their comments. While the Jimmy Carter of the Camp David Accords had been scrupulously neutral in brokering the deal, his success had made him into a defender of Israel in their grade-school memories—and now they were being forced to confront the realization that maybe the Carter of their childhood fantasies had never existed.

It was hard for me to share their disappointment. Because I experienced most of the Carter administration living in Israel and the United Kingdom, I had grown up with a less rosy but more realistic view of his presidential diplomacy. Peace was realpolitik for Carter, not some idealistic crusade, and his role in the process, though significant, did not seem otherworldly to me either. He wasn't a paladin bringing peace, but simply a man in the position to help Sadat and Begin finish what they had started. Or so I had believed at the time.

After our phone interview, though, I wasn't so sure. I was surprised by the risks the soft-spoken, eighty-three-year-old former peanut farmer from Georgia was willing to take. "He's the antithesis of Christian Zionists," I remember telling Lerner afterward. "No wonder right-wing and neoconservative Jews here hate him so much." My boss demurred. Whatever Carter represented to him, he didn't seem comfortable that so much animosity could be directed at the former president. *Tikkun* was being retooled to serve an interfaith readership for which the example of the Camp David Accords could provide crucial common ground. Strategically, the timing of Carter's metamorphosis into a divisive figure was poor indeed. But perhaps our interview could help contain the damage.

I wasn't optimistic. As Lerner hurried off to his next appointment, I predicted that Carter would continue to inspire hostile responses, even from our progressive readership. By using the term "apartheid," the former president had triggered reflexes that were too deep-seated to be stilled by any clarification of his intentions. And, frankly, he hadn't gone out of his way to patch up the wounds his book had inflicted. Instead of seeking to make peace with those he had offended, he seemed more interested in demonstrating how much they had wounded him. What surprised me most was Carter's incredulity that people who once took his peacemaking credentials for granted could now regard him as a hopelessly partisan figure.

From his perspective, it was absolutely clear that both American congressional leaders and the Jewish community were largely responsible for the deterioration of the Israel-Palestine conflict. In settling for what they thought was the status quo, they had actually been sliding inexorably backward, and their refusal to acknowledge their own culpability only made matters worse. Even if Carter were speaking as a man of peace, he was in the throes of a righteous and, indeed, self-righteous anger. He sounded less like the anti-Semite that some of his more vociferous detractors had accused him of becoming than a jilted lover. Why had he been forsaken?

It's easy to understand why Carter would take umbrage. After all, when it comes to peacemaking in the Middle East, it's impossible to imagine a presidential administration more diametrically opposed to his own than that of George W. Bush. Despite the push made at Annapolis in November 2007 to reinvigorate the Arab-Israeli peace process, the differences remained stark. Carter had helped to secure the most comprehensive and lasting agreement between Israel and its historically most threatening neighbor, ushering in a period of relative peace and prosperity in the region. Bush, on the other hand, had invaded Iraq and Afghanistan, in the process helping to prod Israel into its sixth major war and emboldening the nation's most powerful adversary, Iran. From Carter's perspective, anyone taking a long view of the region's history should have no trouble reaching the conclusion that George W. Bush, not he, was the real villain.

The problem, of course, was that the long view was in short supply. Carter's criticisms were a sobering reminder of what the Right would rather deny. Despite his notorious liberalism, Carter was still something of an insider whose public statements mattered to the government of the United States. His use of the term "apartheid" had to be read as a criticism of his own country as much as it was of Israel. If the corollary of the Carter administration's achievements in the Middle East implied that George W. Bush had actually been the worst

American president in Israeli history, a lot of conservative Jews preferred to forget. Right-wing American Jews, both Zionist and neoconservative, didn't want to consider that they might have abetted the Bush administration in damaging Israel's interests and security. For these Jews to be informed of this deeply disturbing argument by a goy—what's more, a sanctimonious Evangelical who builds housing for the poor when he isn't monitoring elections around the world—was too much for their psyches to handle.

We can discern here a companion to *Ha'aretz*'s point that Carter remembers not only what Israel forgets, but also what the U.S. forgets. By refusing to retire to the golf course or park bench like recent Republican presidents, Carter became a thorn in the side of the conservative hegemony of the post–9/11 United States—a thorn that worked its way deeper inside despite the Bush administration's best efforts to act as if American involvement in the Middle East had begun in 2001. The anger he expressed in that *Tikkun* interview may not have seemed very presidential, but it's precisely this energy that made him impossible to ignore.

Without a doubt, the self-aggrandizement that right-wing commentators have accused Carter of demonstrating on his various foreign trips is a part of the package. The former president refused to be embalmed by history—not many former leaders can return to prominence decades after leaving political office. Not only does he remember what others would prefer to forget, he forces us to remember Jimmy Carter in the process.

Regardless of his tendency to court publicity even when it might be better to work behind the scenes,

Carter has a problem actually perceiving himself as a provocateur. By presenting himself as a paladin instead of a pragmatist, he risked falling into the sort of mythological sensibility that *Palestine: Peace, Not Apartheid* implicitly excoriates. If you're going to be a thorn in people's side, you're better off focusing your attention outward instead of on your own injuries.

Reconstructing "Apartheid"

I began this book by describing my daydream of seeing Anwar Sadat speak in place of George W. Bush because I want to advocate an approach to politics that refuses to filter the fantasy out of facts. The concept of a Jimmy Carter who remembers what Israel would prefer to forget depends simultaneously upon treating a person like a metaphor and treating a state like a person. In other words, the argument only makes sense if you allow for literary license. But that doesn't make it any less compelling. On the contrary, such formulations are rooted in the religious and cultural heritage that the United States shares with Israel. References to "Israel" can never be entirely freed from the fantasies that this heritage mobilizes. Israel was a state of mind before it became a physical state.

This point bears heavily on the substance of *Ha'aretz*'s description of the situation in the Occupied Territories: the term "apartheid" is, like "Israel" itself, linguistically ambiguous. Technically, it's an Afrikaans word derived from the Dutch spoken by South African colonists. Although its literal English translation—"apart-hood," or, less strangely, "apartness"—is highly abstract and could refer to a wide range of circumstances, its historical application was highly specific. Apartheid didn't refer to a nebulous sense of difference, but to a political order that systematically denied the rights of nonwhite South Africans. Although state-sponsored demographic inequality is hardly a new historical phenomenon (e.g., the "separate but equal" policies of the segregated American South during the so-called Jim Crow era), apartheid stands out because it lasted so long and became a global issue.

The 1950s and '60s witnessed an unprecedented change of the international political landscape, with almost all of the formerly colonized areas of Africa and Asia becoming autonomous nations. At the same time, developed countries like the U.S. and Australia were making fitful progress toward redressing long-standing historical discrimination against portions of their populations. Whatever the private sentiments of citizens who were negatively affected by these changes (many of whom had difficulty adjusting to the loss of privileges they'd once taken for granted), people around the world were overwhelmingly relieved at the dismantling of "backward" political entities in favor of more civilized ones bound together under the auspices of the United Nations.

But South Africa resisted this trend with a vengeance. Instead of giving in to both internal and external pressure to end white supremacy, the country's leaders strengthened their resolve to maintain the status quo by any means necessary. Because the world depended on South Africa's immense natural resources—including gold, diamonds, and tungsten—this seemingly foolhardy isolationism didn't prove as detrimental as it might have been. Even as the international community prevented South Africa from participating in the United Nations and the Olympics, some of its most prominent members, including the United States, permitted corporations to engage in business-as-usual there.

This glaring double standard inspired a new kind of protest movement, in which citizens worldwide worked to expand South Africa's political isolation into the economic isolation necessary to make its leaders take notice. This social force distinguished itself from precursors such as the American civil rights movement or even the antinuclear movement by the realization that transnational corporations and the governments working on their behalf had radically blurred the distinction between domestic and foreign policy. Taking on apartheid meant taking on the companies that did business in South Africa, even if their operations there were conducted by legally autonomous subsidiaries. Although it wasn't easy at first to articulate the connection between a Bank of America branch in California and the firm's financial holdings in South Africa, activists eventually learned to do the job well enough to meaningfully impact the corporations they targeted. Indeed, this indirect approach—with its accompanying calls for divestment—proved to have more teeth than international sanctions directed at the South African regime.

But this impressive achievement resulted in some curiously unintended consequences. Nelson Mandela's elevation to the status of a political deity made it difficult for people outside South Africa to get a clear sense of what his African National Congress party was actually doing on the ground. It didn't help that Mandela's imprisonment kept him significantly out of touch. The more the international antiapartheid movement grew, the more detached it became from the reality it was meant to confront. Although that syndrome is inevitable for any protest movement that succeeds on an international scale, the ramifications were greatly magnified in this case because most of the protesters had never been to South Africa and had little knowledge of the place.

The fantasy of a different South Africa led to a transformation of the term "apartheid" itself. For many participants in the protest movement, apartheid metamorphosed from a concrete social and political order into an identifier for all that was backward in the world. To the extent that these individuals (many of whom had come to the movement without a clear sense of purpose) were invested in their collective identity as progressives, apartheid became a way to define themselves negatively. In advocating its end, they were also confirming their own status as beings on the pathway to Enlightenment. It's no accident that aging hippies flocked to the antiapartheid movement, and that it became a means for them to establish temporary solidarity with college students with whom they otherwise might have been at odds.

Nelson Mandela's release from prison and his formation of South Africa's first postapartheid government brought great celebration for progressives everywhere. The good guys had won, for once. However vicarious the ensuing feeling of triumph, it proved a potent salve for a Left still smarting from the supposed death of Marxism and the continued vigor of conservative politics throughout the developed world. The desire to bask in that feeling may have deafened many progressives to the bad news emerging from places like the former Yugoslavia and Rwanda, neither of which inspired international protest movements commensurate with their gravity. In a sense, the clarity of the ANC's victory in South Africa may have been almost as damaging to progressive psyches as the clarity of the Eastern bloc's defeat a half decade before. If your identity is principally defined in the negative—as an opponent of discrimination, for example—then it becomes difficult to find your footing in the absence of a clear obstacle to push against.

That's one of the reasons why Israel became the subject of much more intense scrutiny by the global Left in the 1990s. Despite significant differences in the two nations' practices of racism, the fact that they were both European-led settler-states discriminating against indigenous populations made the analogy attractive. Israel (which had already been an important target of European leftists in the late 1960s and early 1970s) found itself in the unenviable position of being a familiar problem in an era that made it difficult for anyone to get his or her political bearings. Ironically enough, many Israeli progressives also took up the struggle against South African apartheid during this period.

The timing of the first Palestinian intifada in 1987—coinciding with the height of the global campaign against South African apartheid—didn't help Israel defy such comparisons. Televised images of Israeli troops shooting unarmed Arab teenagers and South African police firing shotguns at large crowds of young black Africans reinforced the equation. Scale played a role too. Although the antiapartheid movement had done a pretty impressive job of portraying a South African regime sustained by poorly regulated global capitalism, the diluted Marxist theory underpinning the movement's arguments was made palatable by the sense that apartheid was a manageable cause. South Africa is just one country—and Israel is even smaller.

The fact that the Palestinians were once the majority population in historic Palestine helps contribute to the confusion surrounding their situation today, particularly when compared to the way apartheid worked in South Africa, where the indigenous population always constituted the ethnic majority. As a form of discrimination, apartheid described the subjugation of this majority population by a minority. Inside Israel's 1967 borders, the situation has been reversed since the nation's founding. While Israeli conservatives in favor of a two-state solution are fond of speaking about the "demographic threat" created by the occupation—meaning the threat that the "explosive" Palestinian birthrate in the territories and Israel combined will one day create a South Africa–like situation—one cannot say such a demography exists now. This does not mean that the kinds of discrimination practiced against Palestinians in either Israel or the territories are any less deplorable because of it. But they are different enough from what the South African regime did under apartheid to undermine the force of attempts to equate it with Israel.

There is another significant problem with the apartheid analogy. The Europeans who settled sub-Saharan Africa did so under the guise that they were bringing civilization to the region. But the Europeans who settled in Palestine in the nineteenth century conceived of their task in other terms. The Middle East has been the setting for European fantasies since the time of the Crusades. Whether they were religious or secular is less important than the degree to which they were bound to a specific geography rich with history. Western visions of the region—as a place of spiritual fulfillment, of energy wealth, or of national self-realization—have almost always run counter to the general interests of its inhabitants. The same holds true, ironically, for progressives today, who project onto Israel even as they sincerely battle against the legacy of previous Western fantasies of the region.

What these progressives have consistently failed to see is the complex reality of Israel's present-day demographics. Though they regard it as a culturally European state, nearly half the Jewish population is of Arab descent. What are we to make of these Israelis? How can they be deemed "white"—following through on the apartheid analogy—in opposition to Israel's indigenous Palestinian population? They are, as Israeli sociologist Yehuda Shenhav calls them, "Arab Jews," with roots in countries like Algeria, Iraq, Syria, Yemen, and Morocco. At the same time, despite being native to the region, they nevertheless live in a political environment shaped by European colonialism, creating power relations between Middle Eastern Jews and non-Jews that recall the inequalities of the imperial order in Africa and Asia.

The specificity of this dual identity is concealed by attempts to equate the situation in Israel with the one that prevailed in South Africa. Indeed, the analogy renders this significant population of Middle Eastern Jews invisible precisely where its presence most needs to be registered. The insistence that all Israelis are colonists, without regard to their origins, serves to disguise the possibility that Israel suffers from the sort of ethnic and religious conflicts that plague other Middle Eastern countries such as Lebanon and Iraq.

Without diminishing Israel's European roots, the use of the term "apartheid" has the unintended consequence of indulging a way of thinking about the country that discriminates against Jews of regional ancestry, by making them white, like their Ashkenazi coreligionists. This is part of the problem with using religion as though it were a synonym for race, and then repurposing it to describe Jewish racism against Arabs.

INVISIBILITY AS "SEPARATION"

Commentators on the tensions in Israel and Palestine generally focus on how physically close the antagonists are to each other. Like the Troubles in Northern Ireland or the violent breakup of Yugoslavia, this conflict seems to inspire poignant accounts of how the personal becomes political. Families are divided. Neighbors turn against each other after years of living peacefully together. The landscape itself is distorted by walls that make natural boundaries redundant or irrelevant. The NPR report on Christmas celebrations in the Holy Land that I discussed at the end of Chapter Two is typical. Whereas previously such a feature would have highlighted the temporary transcendence of worldly concerns, now it focuses on how impossible that transcendence is. But the emphasis on closeness, however claustrophobic, remains.

This offers a different way of understanding the fetishization of Israel in the Diaspora. As I argued earlier, it's powerfully enhanced by the dual citizenship that Jews around the world enjoy. They invest in Israel both financially and psychologically because it does, in a sense, belong to them. The United States technically belongs to them too, but it doesn't inspire the same type of interest. Even patriotic Americans tend to act as though their participation is unimportant in the grand scheme of things.

With Israel, by contrast, Diaspora Jews sense a stronger ability to make a difference. Indeed, they exhibit more confidence in their capacity to influence Israeli affairs than the people who live there. And that confidence may be somewhat justified given the role that foreign investment plays in the country's political and economic circumstances. What's most interesting is the perception itself rather than its relationship to reality. If Israel seems like a country where individual agency isn't overwhelmed by the inertia of the masses, it becomes much easier to fetishize.

Think of the more concrete and familiar forms of fetish from everyday life. The person who feels power and confidence when they whip out a cigarette lighter, compact, or an iPhone—the best example these days—has found a fetish small enough to manipulate with ease. Filing cabinets resist being fetishized. Virtual files that open and close with a nifty snap on an iPhone screen vigorously invite it. Scale matters more than we think it does.

When it comes to discussing the security situation in Israel, this means that proximity is perceived as both a problem and a solution. The fact that Palestine is mixed up with Israel, in both a geographic and historical sense, makes it far more difficult to separate potentially hostile parties from each other than would be the case in a roomy land like the United States. Had the Indian reservations set up throughout the nineteenth century been located in the midst of heavily populated areas, it would have been much harder to sustain the ideology of Manifest Destiny. But for Israel this condition keeps the conflicts from becoming abstract. The human cost of violence hits too close to home to numb with reason.

Although segregation may produce similar effects in a larger country like the U.S. that it has in Israel, they can be more difficult to perceive in all that vastness. Somehow, a policy dedicated to keeping people apart seems more absurd and unjustified when its scale is reduced to a psychologically manageable scope. The "apartheid" label sticks to Israel for just this reason. The "economic apartheid" that some progressive activists have used to describe impoverished areas of the United States is a much harder sell than its Israeli equivalent because there's so much more room to maneuver.

INVESTING IN ISRAEL

It was a tiny, poorly ventilated room with a clear view of the vast, produce-filled store floor below. Every seat at the table was already taken, except for two spots reserved for the event's speakers: myself and Rabbi Michael Lerner, who was widely considered at the time to be one of America's most outspoken Jewish critics of Israeli foreign policy. We had arrived to participate in a debate over whether the Rainbow Grocery, San Francisco's largest organic supermarket, ought to boycott Israeli products to protest the country's treatment of the Palestinians.

In response to the decision by two of the cooperative members to pull Israeli products from their sections of the store earlier that year, Rainbow's staff had decided to wage a vigorous internal discussion about whether or not it should formally undertake such a measure as a politically concerned business. Already the subject of intense Jewish scrutiny, Lerner and I were invited to explain to the embattled grocery why we didn't think a boycott would work.

As honored as I was to be invited in tandem with Lerner, I was concerned that his positions—progressive as they might seem in other contexts—would appear too conservative for Rainbow's well-educated leftist employees. Sure enough, Lerner fulfilled my expectations. He began to argue that since Jews had been the targets of numerous Christian-derived boycotts throughout history, the threat of a new one would only stiffen resolve in the Diaspora to support the occupation.

The audience grew restive, as evinced by the impatient and in some cases exasperated looks directed at Lerner during the Q&A session that followed. Considering the increasingly dire circumstances Palestinians were facing in 2003, our listeners didn't want to be implored to show greater sensitivity to the history of Jewish suffering. With the IDF reoccupying the West Bank, stepping up targeted assassinations, and making it increasingly difficult for Palestinians to support themselves, it must have felt like a bait-and-switch to be asked to remember that the oppressors were descended from the victims of oppression.

As the rabbi and members of Rainbow's staff went back and forth, I realized how little headway he was making with his audience. They weren't coming to an understanding—at best, they were confirming the belief that public debate is a good thing, no matter the outcome. When Lerner finally got up to leave, sighing, I surveyed the crowd. Sizing up how raw everyone was feeling, I decided to take a different tack. Rather than invoke a well-worn historical argument, I decided to come out as an Israeli with a strong sense of what was going on in the country on the ground. I would try to engage them casually in a way that someone like Lerner—who preferred to address his audiences in a formal manner— would not.

I noted that even Israelis found the return to warfare irrational, and spoke about the difficulties that the fighting was imposing upon the country's overall economy, going so far as to cite the hardships my own family was undergoing at the time. Shifting gears, I proposed that the U.S. invasion of Iraq the month before had introduced an entirely new level of complexity to the situation that would soon challenge the Left to come up with brand-new ways to help settle the Israel-Palestine conflict. For now, Israel had won, and the American presence in the region only served to reinforce that.

By emphasizing such issues, I hoped to give the impression that there's no single progressive "Jewish" approach to discussing the situation. More ambitiously, I wanted to appeal to our audience's concerns about globalization by emphasizing the importance of political economy and imperialism in properly analyzing the forces at play in the conflict. I figured that since talking about the singularity of Jewish history failed to persuade them, it wouldn't hurt to introduce other kinds of discourses about the Middle East, particularly coming from someone who holds Israeli citizenship and also speaks the language of the American Left.

Although the second half of the discussion was a little warmer, some differences proved too difficult to bridge. Inevitably, the term "apartheid" was brought up and became the focus of intense debate. One person who was wearing a T-shirt with Arabic writing emphasized the term, calling Israel an "apartheid state." I took issue, saying that this was more of an apt description of the situation in the Occupied Territories than in Israel proper. Another older person who identified herself as a Jew who'd grown up in South Africa during the apartheid era gave me one of those "you can't be serious" looks and politely disagreed, explaining that she'd spent time in Israel and couldn't see any serious difference. I tried to clarify how complex the official practice of anti-Arab discrimination in Israel actually is, but by that point the conversation had almost ground to a halt. Tempers had flared too much to make it worthwhile to continue.

This unfortunate conclusion to what had been a fruitful, if frustrating, discussion confirmed for me just how divisive the term "apartheid" can be. Perhaps if Jimmy Carter had spent time in that sort of conversation, he would have used the word more cautiously in the course of making arguments that would stand on their own without such a contentious label. But I also came away with a visceral sense of how much Israel's activity can matter to people who have little investment in its future, whether financially or psychologically. While some participants in the debate, such as the woman from South Africa, identified themselves as Jewish, the majority saw no reason to specify their ethnic heritage. They took it for granted that Israel's treatment of Palestinians was a political topic worth their personal attention.

This realization might seem depressing. After all, as the audience's response to Rabbi Lerner indicated, being passionate about an issue is often the same thing as having made up one's mind about it. The back and forth of the Q&A session might have been illuminating, but it still testified to a significant distance between viewpoints. Even so, I didn't leave the meeting depressed— on the contrary, the fact that so many people cared to come and participate struck me as a hopeful sign. To be sure, American interest in Israel is frequently self-serving in that the Israel-Palestine conflict holds appeal for progressives who are overwhelmed by the scale of problems closer to home. While their investment signals an impulse to fetishize, with all that implies, the fact that the investment is there at all means that it can be mobilized for different, more productive ends.

SPEAKING IN CODE

The controversy over the use of the term "apartheid" indicates that we lack an accurate language with which to talk about or describe the moral problems raised by Israel's occupation of the West Bank and Gaza. It's also a sign of the discrepancies that exist within Jewish political experience in the Diaspora, where Jews may be socially and politically progressive as Americans, but less so in matters pertaining to Israel. Maybe the hysteria in Jewish American reactions to the apartheid charge demonstrates their concern about how it reflects on Jewish American politics more than what it says about Israeli politics. After all, Israelis themselves are likelier to use the term to describe the kind of colonial domination being practiced in the Occupied Territories than their American counterparts.

"Apartheid" has an aura in the Diaspora that it lacks in Israel proper. Among other things, this means that when *Ha'aretz* used the term in its editorial about the disrespect shown Jimmy Carter, they were courting more trouble with their international and primarily Englishlanguage readership than they were domestically. The biggest reason for this is at least superficially counterintuitive. To someone who's intimately familiar with actually existing Israel, the territories, or what counts as the Palestinian nation, it's abundantly clear where the term "apartheid" misses its mark. Indeed, it can seem almost quaint given how complex the situation on the ground really is.

Palestinians are subject to forms of control that extend far beyond efforts to separate them physically from Jews. In fact, despite partitioning of the land, Jewish and Arab life remain radically intertwined. The problem of proximity introduced into everyday life by the region's population density makes whatever separation or "apartness" that is imposed on the landscape—through walls, bypass roads, and checkpoints—only part of the story. While the same could be said for the reality of apartheid in certain portions of South Africa, such as the Johannesburg area, it was ultimately a far more primitive system. What the South African regime managed to do with brute force and in a much more expansive territory, Israel has had to approximate with a wide range of techniques that run the gamut from crude to subtle.

Israel's dubious achievement is that it has devised a strategy for maintaining power over the Palestinians that's more insidious than the South African model of apartheid because it operates on so many different levels at once.

To an Israeli, the term "apartheid" may seem morally useful despite the fact that it only serves to explain one aspect of the treatment of Palestinians. Although the word may denote the more visible and less sophisticated aspects of the Israeli government's approach to security, it's a limited metaphor. But it is valuable precisely because of how much it reveals the limits of a certain brand of political thinking. So long as the people who use the word recognize this, "apartheid" can be drained of the almost supernatural force that has been ascribed to it in the Diaspora.

But, unfortunately, the increasing interpenetration of Israel and the Diaspora has made that task more difficult. Consider the cold shoulder that Israel's leaders gave to Jimmy Carter on his April 2008 visit: it reflected an eagerness not to placate Israeli conservatives, but to honor the consternation the ex-president had provoked in the Diaspora. If Israeli leaders go through the motions of maintaining a firm stance for Jews outside Israel rather than for those to whom security is an immediate concern, then the political climate has been corrupted to an unprecedented degree. The reflexes apparent in the Diaspora, particularly in the United States, are ones that Israelis adopt at their peril.

Political vocabulary isn't the same as political action, but it does help to determine that action. It makes historical sense that the term "apartheid" was applied to

Israel's treatment of Palestinians. Progressives simply did not have a language to describe the nature of that relationship, so they turned to the best analogy they could find. But along the way, too many of them forgot that they were making a provisional and decidedly imperfect comparison. Instead of helping to focus attention on specific aspects of Israel's approach to security, the term "apartheid" ended up diffusing the critique.

THE LAST WORD FOR RACISM

It is important to bear in mind that this counterproductive trend was already underway before the term "apartheid" was widely applied to an Israeli context. Even when apartheid was still the official state policy of South Africa, many people on the Left were inspired to apply it more generally.

One particularly noteworthy instance of such usage involved the French philosopher Jacques Derrida. At the height of his international fame in the early 1980s, Derrida contributed an essay to the catalog for a major exhibition organized by the Association of Artists of the World against Apartheid. Inspired by the stated goal of this project, which was to create a sort of museum for later donation to South Africa's first postapartheid government, Derrida made a play on the idea of there being a "last word" on racism. His essay begins boldly (which is surprising for a thinker who's famous for discerning the subtleties of language): "Apartheid—may that remain the name for now on, the unique appellation for the ultimate racism in the world, the last of many." Although Derrida goes on to explain in depth his reasons for there being a "last word" (*le dernier mot* in French), he never closes the huge opening created by this first sentence.

Indeed, later in the essay, he complicates and reinforces his claim that apartheid designates an ultimate racism by asking: "But hasn't *apartheid* always been the archival record of the unnameable?" Derrida seems to wants us to think of this "last word" as simultaneously historical and transcendental. Apartheid in South Africa may represent an end of the line for a certain mode of state-sponsored racism, but as a term it also serves as a substitute for what can't be named. The analogy to the deity of the Torah, who can only be represented indirectly, is clear.

Derrida's Jewish heritage is manifest here. Although outwardly secular like the vast majority of postwar European intellectuals, he was repeatedly drawn to meditations on the limits of language that reflect a long-standing concern in Judaism with the problem of naming. If he errs on the side of generalization in this essay, he does so self-consciously, aware of the existential burden that falls on whomever steps into Adam's shoes. He also makes this move mindful of the most radical example of modern racism, Nazi Germany's program to root out "foreign" elements in its population. "The word [*apartheid*] occupies the terrain like a concentration camp," he declares midway through the essay. "System of partition, barbed wire, crowds of mapped-out solitudes."

Significantly, he immediately follows this sidelong invocation of the Holocaust by further speculating on the abstract power of the term "apartheid." Derrida states that it "concentrates separation, raises it to an-

other power and sets separation itself *apart*." The word's
euphemistic quality—"apartness" is an absurdly vague
concept—helps illustrate a point about the nature of discrimination. He concludes: "There's no racism without a
language. The point is not that acts of racial violence are
only words but rather that they have to have a word."
It's a compelling argument, particularly for someone
seeking to group different forms of social and political
discrimination together. Racism has to have a word, but
so does the critique of racism. Why not *apartheid*?

The problem is that this transformation of one instance of state-sponsored racism into a surrogate for all
brands of state-sponsored racism threatens to obscure
the facts about apartheid as it actually functioned in
South Africa.

That was certainly the angle taken by South African
scholars Anne McClintock and Rob Nixon, who wrote
a harsh yet fair-minded critique of Derrida's essay, to
which he in turn made a rather condescending reply. Patiently explaining the risk in letting his "diffuse historical comments" stand in for a more concrete engagement
with the subject of apartheid, McClintock and Nixon argue that Derrida's well-meaning protest is "deficient in
any sense of how the discourses of South African racism
have at once been historically constituted and politically
constitutive." In his haste to have the "last word" on the
language of racism, Derrida "blurs historical differences
by conferring on the single term *apartheid* a spurious autonomy and agency." That is, he's so intent on theoriz-
ing the term that he fails to recognize that even in its native South Africa, it reduces complexities to the flatness
of slogan. "Derrida," they conclude, "allows the solitary

word *apartheid* to absorb so much of his attention that the changing discourses of South African racism appear more monolithic than they really are."

AN ABSENCE OF METAPHORS

I draw attention to this exchange both because of the way it resonated with progressive American intellectuals at the time and because it illustrates the pitfalls of relying on a historically specific term like "apartheid." If applying it to the situation in '80s South Africa was as risky as McClintock and Nixon suggest in their critique of Derrida, imagine how much more potential for confusion its use holds in other contexts. Indeed, the extreme generalizations that Derrida used to argue for racism's "last word" seem mild compared to the ones used today by well-meaning progressives who speak of Israel as an "apartheid state."

Progressives who use this term demonstrate a troubling refusal to develop a political vocabulary adequate to the situation. I wouldn't belittle the passion of advocates for social justice in Israel by calling their fixation on apartheid lazy. But I do think that the inability to describe the situation there precisely—often due to a lack of experience of life on the ground in Israel or Palestine—ends up producing the same effects. Just as it was crucial for antiapartheid activists to understand the historical and ideological uniqueness of state-managed discrimination in South Africa, the same level of specificity is required to make headway toward a more equitable treatment of Palestinians, whether they live in Israel, Gaza, or the West Bank. And it's just as important for holding the global Left's anti-Semitic tendencies in check. Even the terms "Israeli" and "Palestinian" feel hopelessly vague at times, concealing as they do the ethnic, religious, and linguistic diversity of the region. Surely, even though Israel isn't Lebanon or Iraq, we'd still do well to learn from the more nuanced forms of demographic classification that we've applied to the populations of those countries.

The tragic irony of the occupation is that Israel is inadvertently creating an approximation of the Europe that the Jews were forced to leave behind, one which they continue to inhabit mostly as ghosts. Through their forced resettlement and their proscribed routes of travel, Palestinians have become a similarly spectral presence in Israel. And yet the area's population density guarantees that their ghostly absence exists in close proximity to their physical presence. The Palestinian people are still very much there, even in those places where security measures or economic circumstances have rendered them invisible, reminding us of their presence through acts of resistance as peaceable as building homes without the hard-to-come-by permits, and as violent as suicide bombings.

Though Palestinians are granted rights and elect representatives to their own government, they do not live in a separate country. Even in the Occupied Territories, they've lived in what the army and the settlers have increasingly defined as Israel. Yet as de facto Israeli subjects, they remain (for want of a better term) stateless, lacking in even the most basic rights granted to Palestinian Israelis living on the "Israeli" side of the original 1967 border. In effect, Palestinians are colonial subjects of a state in which there are no colonies, the victims of an imperialism that due to space and policy constraints has been forced to double back on itself, expanding the reach of Israel within the land it already controls. They continue to live in a Jewish country in which Arabs are legally disadvantaged, but can still attain varying degrees of citizenship depending on how far inland they live from the Mediterranean.

Israel is multicultural, but not officially. It's a descriptive rather than a legislative or political multiculturalism, one you can only comprehend on the ground. On paper, Palestinian welfare is delegated to a separate, incomplete government that has existed off and on with varying levels of effectiveness, but whose sovereignty is always at the pleasure of Israel. However, the Palestinians who live under what amounts to a dual government are not the whole story. Much to the chagrin of right-wingers, Israel's own Palestinian population is not only visible but also obviously growing. Every major Israeli city has Palestinian neighborhoods, and the country contains numerous Palestinian towns—particularly in the north, where the majority of the Palestinian population within Israel's pre-1967 borders resides. Go to any major commercial area in the region, and you're bound to hear Arabic in Jewish-owned stores, or see Palestinian women wearing hijab as they shop for groceries or clothes, or stop at cafés to socialize.

Palestinian invisibility is therefore decidedly relative, their absence in some contexts countered by a presence in others. The effect of this status is to render right-wing arguments on behalf of separation—or even annexation—of the Occupied Territories suspect for their alleged "inclusiveness," and to reveal left-wing contentions about the totalizing character of Israel's practice of apartheid seem hopelessly crude. The fact of the matter is that in Israel both multiculturalism and what is inaccurately termed "apartheid" are imbricated with other more subtle forms of domination, making it folly to attempt to reduce the entirety of Israeli society's structure to one overriding ethnic principle; there are, indeed, many such principles vying for ideological hegemony. The problem, really, is that this diversity coexists alongside what remains an extremely brutal colonial occupation of the West Bank, one which many analysts believe has grown harsher and more complex over the years, in some instances transcending, in terms of its cruelty, the sort of enforced separation signaled by the term "apartheid." As Israeli architect-cum–critical theorist Eyal Weizman argues, Israel has innovated a number of new forms of domination in the Occupied Territories that seem more nuanced and far-reaching, in terms of space, architecture, and geography, than their predecessors from the heyday of international colonialism.

I don't propose that progressives seek a more muted political vocabulary. The condition of the Palestinian people is too dire to worry about pushing the buttons of moderates who aren't sure where they stand on the way Israel treats them. Undoubtedly, something has to be done both internally and externally to set the peace process in motion on more equitable terms. That is, after all, why Jimmy Carter visited Israel in April 2008. But a term like "apartheid" conceals more than it reveals and can only be counterproductive. The former president's efforts to defend himself and his reasoned positions prove that it's a needless distraction at a time when we should be conserving our strength for other, more pressing struggles.

Chapter Five

A DESPERATE EMBRACE

In the weeks immediately following the terrorist attacks of September 11, 2001, some of the most frequent guests on American news programs were Israeli diplomats and security consultants who were asked to share their battle-hardened wisdom on the tragedy. In interview after interview, it was like they were all reading from the same script: Now America knows what it's like to be subject to Islamic terrorism. Now America understands that we're struggling against the same enemy. Now America understands why it must support Israel in its fight against Arafat, because behind him stands Osama bin Laden.

The most disconcerting thing about these talking heads' commentary was how calculated it appeared to be. The U.S. had just weathered the first attack on its soil since Pearl Harbor, and Americans of all political stripes were in a state of shock. Yet these Israeli experts were less interested in providing solace than spin. Like the hardheaded businessman who sees opportunity in a competitor's misfortune, they seemed almost happy to have the perfect talking point in their efforts to shore up American support for their fight against the Palestinians. And their composure amid the overwhelming confusion of the attacks' aftermath paid handsome dividends. Soon, television networks were broadcasting scenes of jubilant Palestinians celebrating al-Qaeda's attacks on the streets of Nablus and Ramallah, as if to confirm everything their Israeli guests were saying.

For conspiracy theorists searching for evidence that Israel prodded the United States to invade Iraq, it's hard to imagine better proof. Unless, of course, those television networks used file footage of Palestinians shot years before 9/11 in some of these segments, as later turned out to be the case. Plenty of people on both the Right and Left—even if they dismiss the more far-fetched scenarios, such as the Mossad orchestrating the attacks—are readily persuaded by the apparent proof of Israel's undue influence on the mainstream media. Any short-term benefits those Israelis achieved by urging Americans to follow their country's example could never make up for the long-term damage wrought by their words. Considering that most Americans would have likely seen the Israeli perspective more favorably without such insufferable goading, it was a grave strategic error to reinforce the already widespread stereotype that Israelis—and Jews—will ruthlessly pursue their own interests even in the face of massive suffering. The worldwide resurgence and global persistence of anti-Semitism is alarming enough. Helping it along in this way is madness.

Why did these Israelis repeat the same points over and over, seemingly without worrying about their consequences? How could their testimony have come off so well coordinated? The answers lay in the peculiar nature of Israel's relationship with the United States. In both

countries, government officials and their allies in aca-
demia and the media are so practiced in going through
the motions of showing how deeply committed they are
to each other, even in the face of superficial disagree-
ment, that they know precisely what they're expected to
say in any given situation. As the 2008 American presidential campaign powerfully reminded us, even politicians who stake their future on a platform of change
struggle to resist the status quo when the topic turns to
Israel. If anything, this sense of clearly defined limits is
stronger still on the Israeli side of the equation. Those
"experts" were simply doing what they and their predecessors had been trained to do: reminding Americans
that their fate is inextricably bound up with Israel's. Although there had never been a more obvious occasion
to deviate from the script, they lacked both the will and
way to do so.

It wasn't just a question of respecting the special
circumstances in the United States, either. While Israel
obviously needed to show sympathy for what its partner was going through, the timing was ripe for a thor-
ough reconsideration of the two nations' relationship,
not a retrenchment. By strengthening the link between
Israel's struggles and those of the U.S., Israeli conservatives acted as though they were caught up in a destructive
love affair: when they felt threatened by the possibility of
freedom, they did everything they could to repeat past
mistakes, as if they hoped that ritual itself could stave
off forces of change. For whatever reason, they were
either unwilling or unable to see that despite Israel's
long-standing strategic alliance with the U.S., it was a
huge mistake for Israel to blur the distinction between

its own conflicts with the Arab world and those of its partner. Israel's conflicts were relatively contained and far more localized than the ones the U.S. was already planning in the wake of 9/11. At peace with Egypt and Jordan and having just withdrawn from Lebanon in May 2000, Israel needed to keep its focus on the second Palestinian uprising. Certainly, the last thing the Jewish state needed was to add to its already impressive collection of enemies.

You don't have to be a Middle East scholar to understand why members of the Israeli political establishment were inclined to view 9/11 as an occasion to renew their special relationship with the United States. These terrorist attacks, carried out by Arabs as an explicit response to American foreign and military policies in the Middle East—particularly since the first Gulf War—had temporarily given Americans a chance to experience what they had previously learned about from afar. At a time when financial and military support for Israel had become less attractive outside of Washington, D.C., this tragic event threatened to dispel most people's questions about the use of American resources. Israel could point to its success at preventing terrorist attacks of a similar scale to retroactively justify all the money and equipment it had received from the United States. "Security doesn't come cheap" would serve as the perfect rallying cry.

The post–9/11 political landscape gave Israel a chance to maintain the high-level intimacy with the U.S. that had prevailed during the Clinton years and was feared to be in danger of cooling off under a new, potentially less friendly Republican administration. What better opportunity to renew the emotional bonds between the two countries—and to maintain the military and economic ties—than to alert the American public to a growing Islamist threat that was no longer restricted to Israel. Israelis were happy to tell Americans that the anger directed against them was not the fault of American-led sanctions on Iraq, American support for authoritarian regimes, or American control of Middle Eastern oil. The problem, they would say (barely containing their I-told-you-so impulse), was one they all shared: a history of ethnic conflict that cast both Jews and Americans as reviled Westerners.

What went unspoken in this commentary was how much Israel needed U.S. political support. Though Israel's conflicts with neighboring states were contained, its struggle with the Palestinians was raging in 2001. The Israeli security apparatus had seen the country's withdrawal from Lebanon in 2000 as a rehearsal for leaving the Occupied Territories—and was stunned when the Oslo peace process failed. With the al-Aksa Intifada, Israel saw itself as having no choice but to hitch its wagon to American efforts to combat Islamic terrorism and impose a new regional Pax Americana. The model would be America's victory over Iraq in 1991, which helped push the Palestinians and Syria toward the negotiating table. In this hypothetical scenario, whatever wasn't accomplished by negotiations would be imposed by force, with Israel continuing its counterinsurgency campaign against the Palestinians and the United States waging all-out war on any regional powers providing material and financial support to the new Palestinian resistance.

Called upon as America's most militarily powerful ally in the Middle East, Israel did everything in its power to support the Bush administration's new strategic doctrine in the region. The problem with the position that Israel took, however, was that it gave little thought to the possibility that America might not prevail politically or militarily over its adversaries as it had in both the first Gulf War and, more importantly, the Cold War. Nor did Israel adequately consider how its alliance with the United States might constrain its ability to make decisions on its own behalf, without having to prioritize American interests over its own.

As the years since 9/11 have demonstrated, the renewed relationship between Israel and the U.S. during the Bush era was in fact a desperate embrace in which each party's attempt to gain strength from the other only exposed the weak points in their special relationship. Every new crisis created by the War on Terror managed to bring out the worst in both nations. Like codependents they ended up enabling each other's authoritarian and antidemocratic tendencies, looking to their partner to justify actions that were highly unpopular outside of their respective borders. Unfortunately, this dangerous trend was powerfully abetted by failures in both nations' intelligence and diplomatic communities. Military and economic realities that had emerged in the Middle East since President Clinton first took office still hadn't been properly analyzed. Under the banner of the War on Terror, the United States and Israel made crucial decisions on the basis of bad information.

BACK TO THE FUTURE

It was a cold Friday night in the winter of 1994. As we sipped sweet cups of black Turkish coffee and nibbled

pieces of baklava my father had brought home from Nazareth, the dinner conversation in my parents' Tel Aviv
apartment turned predictably toward politics. "Personally, I'm relieved that we're finally moving to a conclusion
with the Palestinians," erupted one of our guests. "Now
we'll be able to devote our efforts to the Iranian problem."
All of a sudden, chairs were pushed back, throats were
cleared, and a dreadfully awkward silence ensued, only
to be broken by my savvy stepmother telling our guests
that more coffee was available for those who wanted it.
Still, the palpable discomfort that had flooded the room
remained, giving an edge to the rest of the gathering.

Why was everyone so upset? At that moment, I
finally understood how much emotional investment
we had all made in the peace process, how forcefully
we had imbued it with the messianic power to bring
about an end to the Arab-Israeli conflict. Granted, this
was only the beginning of the Oslo period. It had been
just four months since the signing of the Declaration of
Principles in Washington, D.C., and the initiation of a
formal peace treaty with Jordan was still months away.
Nevertheless, it felt like a new zeitgeist was upon us.
Enough concrete progress had already been made that
an unabashedly utopian optimism felt warranted. Our
guest's faux pas was to remind us of the militaristic realpolitik that both dominated Israel during the decades of
hostilities and achieved success by staying several steps
ahead of its opponents. Debating the next target felt too
much like the old Israel. We were giddy with visions of
an Israel in which the concerns of peace would trump the
cause of war.

Washing up afterward, I reflected on the blood-

bath then underway in Bosnia. The unbelievable brutality of the conflict there contradicted the images of
prodemocracy forces laying nonviolent siege to Eastern
bloc regimes. The new spirit of freedom that had soared
in the overthrow of Communism was now giving way
to the sobering realization that the desire for political
autonomy could not be restricted to the borders established after World War II. Separatist impulses rooted
in deeply felt (if historically dubious) forms of identity
politics were proving stronger than the admonition to
slow the forces of change. It felt like a B-movie version of
the French Revolution. The headway toward a peaceful
resolution of the Israel-Palestine conflict thus provided
a welcome respite—like stories about Nelson Mandela's
ascendancy in South Africa—from news that old conflicts might actually be reinforced by the instability of
what George W. Bush's father famously proclaimed to
be a "New World Order."

It's strange to be nostalgic for a moment of sobering
reevaluation. But the 2000s have made the 1990s look
a lot kinder and gentler than they actually were. Back
then, the United States completely ignored Rwanda,
made a mess of Somalia, grossly underestimated the rise
of transnational terrorist organizations like al-Qaeda,
and only belatedly intervened in the former Yugoslavia. America consistently focused its attention on the
wrong people and the wrong places. But, for all that, the
effects of the West's foreign policy mistakes remained
localized. To be sure, that containment intensified the
violence in the places where it broke out—like an infec-
tion that stays confined to one area, the pain seemed
externally manageable.

Now, though, we are on the verge of global sepsis.
Local problems of the previous decade have spread to
the point where the healthy portions of the world are
in the minority. And the situation in the Middle East,
which seemed to be on the verge of long-lasting change
for the better in 1994, is now as precarious as it has
ever been. Indeed, from Pakistan, which has made its
capabilities public, to Israel, which continues to keep
what everyone knows a secret, to Iran, which has been
working diligently to join the club, nuclear proliferation
in West Asia has made it the most likely catalyst for a
worldwide catastrophe.

That Israel and the Palestinians concluded the final
month of the Bush era with a brutal war in the most
densely populated area of the world, the Gaza Strip,
confirmed what a perfectly precarious situation George
W. Bush was leaving behind in the Middle East. So much
for the propagandistic value of the troop "surge" in
Iraq. If Bush's tenure in office did not really begin until
9/11—unless you consider the clearing of brush for photo
ops a presidential pursuit—it made poetic sense that it
would conclude with the most profound violence that
the Middle East had witnessed since the U.S. invaded
Iraq in March 2003. Whatever the United States had accomplished in the region was evidently not enough to
prevent Israel from finding it necessary to undertake
such action.

This helps to explain the ferocity of Israel's winter
offensive against Hamas. It was a direct reflection of
how much had changed in the Middle East during the
Bush era, and how fearful Israel had become about the
situation. With a new American administration about to

take office—one which had repeatedly indicated, much to Israeli chagrin, that it would prefer to engage in dialogue with Iran despite the country's overt hostility toward Israel and its pursuit of nuclear weapons—the interregnum before Barack Obama's inauguration must have struck Israeli leaders as the last possible opportunity to act without restraint.

Prevented from attacking Iran directly, something even the Bush administration had ruefully forbidden, the next best option was to do as much damage to Hamas as possible. For the Bush administration—which had, on numerous occasions, considered encouraging such an Israeli operation—an attack on Gaza was the best possible last-minute compromise. Predictably, the outgoing White House gave the green light for the operation without hesitation.

The consequences for Israel and its special relationship with the U.S. are grave, even if the leaders of both nations have largely practiced a policy of denial. Ever since the beginning of the Oslo period, supporters of the peace process in Israel and the Diaspora alike have overlooked—whether out of ignorance or simply because of Israel's historic alliance with the United States—the impact of America's post–Cold War foreign policy toward the Islamic world. As legitimate as it might be to argue that a just resolution of the Palestinian-Israeli conflict would have a profound impact on the West's relationship with Middle Eastern states, it's no longer sufficient to place the sole responsibility for regional peace on Palestinians and Israelis. The burden now lies as much on the United States as it does on Israel. During his June 4, 2009, speech in Cairo, President Obama appeared cognizant of this necessity, acknowledging the CIA's role in overthrowing Iran's democratically elected government in 1953, describing the invasion of Iraq a "war of choice," while touching upon the suffering of the Palestinian people and affirming their right to statehood.

That isn't to imply that things would have been easy in an alternate reality in which the United States did not invade Afghanistan and Iraq. Even if the Palestinians and the Israelis had managed to conclude a final status agreement by the year 2000, it would still have been difficult to imagine a Middle East in which a confrontation between Israel and Iran could be avoided. In that respect, my parents' pragmatic guest had been right, even if he did manage to spoil everyone's dessert. Throughout Israel's occupation of southern Lebanon, Iran waged an increasingly sophisticated proxy war against Israel through the Shia guerilla organization Hezbollah, one that has continued in fits and starts throughout the 2000s. Hezbollah slowly gained leverage, which has in turn emboldened its patron's posturing with Sunni clients such as Hamas. As Iran slowly regained the strength that had been sapped in its brutal war with Iraq throughout the 1980s, it began to reassert itself as a regional power. Taking the long view, it's therefore clear that Israel and Iran were already on a collision course long before 9/11.

But if the U.S. can't be blamed for the actual conflict, it's certainly responsible for both accelerating its pace and exponentially increasing the seriousness of the consequences if it eventually comes to a head. Since his election in 2005, Iran's President Mahmoud Ahmadinejad has made confronting Israel one of the central planks of his country's foreign policy. Uttering a succession of hateful pronouncements denying the historical validity of the Holocaust, Ahmadinejad has made abundantly clear his desire to wipe Israel off the map. Would he have come to power in the absence of an American military presence on Iran's eastern and western borders? Many experts on the region believe that if the U.S. had been able to devote its financial and political resources to supporting moderate forces in Iran, a different government would have emerged in his stead. And it's evident that even if Ahmadinejad had nonetheless managed to become president, his courage to provoke Israel, Europe, and the United States would have been constrained without the twin examples of Afghanistan and Iraq.

Though countless pundits contend that Ahmadinejad has chosen to renew hostility toward Israel simply because he subscribes to the anti-Western ideology made famous by the Iranian Revolution, they fail to appreciate the magnitude of recent changes to the region. Iran has refocused its sights on Israel because it's an easy scapegoat for American imperialist policies. To be sure, Israel has always served this purpose to an extent, standing in previously for European powers like Great Britain and France. Israel is never simply Israel, even for those who seem most single-mindedly bent on its destruction. Indeed, the question of scale that I mentioned earlier in discussing international activists' investment in the Israel-Palestine conflict is also a crucial factor in regional hostility toward Israel, whether Arab or Persian.

While it's almost impossible to imagine truly destroying the United States (instead of just wounding it), the idea of eradicating Israel altogether appears less far-fetched. If Israel could drive much of the Palestinian population into exile in 1948 and hold the remainder in political limbo indefinitely, why couldn't the same fate befall the Israelis? Such musings ignore the obvious, which is that the U.S. and its Western allies would never let it happen. In fantasy, however, the smallness of Israel creates a fetish for both Arabs and Americans. The only difference is that it serves a positive or ambiguous function for the latter, while it's entirely negative for the former. On a certain level Israelis know this, which is why politicians such as current Prime Minister Benjamin Netanyahu find it so useful to brandish the threat of an Iranian-provoked nuclear holocaust. The idea that Tehran might be planning such a future for Israel is used to terrorize Israelis as much as it is to attract the sympathy of the outside world.

It is worth noting that fetishes only do their magic when they actually exist. Even the Arabs who believe with all their heart that they want to destoy Israel would suffer severe psychological disruptions if their dream were to come true. Paradoxically, they need Israel to survive in order to stabilize their worldview. An analogy to what happened in Iraq after Saddam Hussein was toppled from power is entirely appropriate here: so long as the majority of the country's population—Shia, Sunni, and Kurd alike—were waiting intently for his removal, everyday life proceeded in a relatively normal fashion, even with the often extreme burdens imposed by the sanctions that followed the first Gulf War. Once Hussein was no longer a focus for their animus, however, they turned on each other. The pent-up rage they went on to express in gruesome displays was too strong to dissipate in the brief period of relief that followed Hussein's ouster.

Regimes such as the one in Iran need Israel to give the people they rule—many of whom are destitute due to systematic economic and political discrimination—an external object for their anger. Not only is the U.S. far too large to serve this fetishistic function, but the reach of its consumer culture, particularly in the form of movies and popular music, makes it hard to regard America as fully external. In a sense, the U.S. is too near even when it's thousands of miles away. By contrast, Israel is a place that people throughout the Middle East can imagine reaching in a geographical sense—the testing of missiles is always reported together with their cruising range—but it's not part of their domestic experience. This has made it a fine scapegoat for the entirety of its six-decade existence.

What has changed since 9/11 and the wars in Afghanistan and Iraq is that the political psychology of the region has been shaken by the physical proximity of American forces. Just as Israel has had to come to terms with the fact that the United States is now a virtual geographic neighbor, Saudi Arabia, Egypt, Syria, and, above all, Iran have had to deal with the repercussions of a military imperialism as invasive as the cultural sort that preceded it. The American presence in the region has never been so thoroughly embodied. For this reason, the old standby of hostility toward Israel is being summoned, often hysterically, as a way to shore up the cracks in these countries' political identities.

Until now, this phenomenon has been most readily apparent in Iran because of its location between the pincers of American military engagement in the region. Considering this physical proximity with the United

States and the Bush administration's blustery rhetoric about extending regime change throughout the region, it's no wonder that Ahmadinejad has amassed political capital by making Israel the fall guy for America's policy failings in the Middle East.

WE CARE A LOT

George W. Bush's May 2008 address to the Knesset was an event that held a little significance for everyone: for Israelis because of the president's reiterated commitment to their security; for Americans because he forcefully critiqued his country's opposition in a foreign parliament; and for Iranians because he reminded them that despite how poorly the U.S. had been faring in Iraq and Afghanistan, it would still protect Israel from any manner of threat. In other words, it was an exercise in consistency, one that a besieged Prime Minister Ehud Olmert duly noted by nearly falling asleep during the speech.

Although the mainstream American media made much of Bush's thinly veiled dig at Barack Obama during his address, it was par for the course. If nothing else, his administration proved that some Republicans are willing to turn any occasion into an opportunity for partisanship. The unwritten rule of Cold War politics—that both Republicans and Democrats were supposed to minimize their differences when they went abroad—had been abandoned years before. Given the dramatic importance that Republicans had attached to securing Jewish votes in the presidential election campaign, Bush's move made sense. Of course the president would take advantage of the situation. But in doing so, he demonstrated just how misguided his administration's policies in the Middle East had been. This situation could not have been more clearly underscored by the fact that 78 percent of America's registered Jewish voters ended up casting their ballots for Barack Obama. In going through the motions of restating the U.S. commitment to Israel to score political points back home, Bush made it obvious that he was either unable or unwilling to acknowledge the deteriorating situation in the Middle East for what it truly had become: a legacy of American failure.

Consider the circumstances at the time of his Knesset speech: by early 2008, it was apparent that the U.S. was slowly but surely losing Lebanon to Iran despite immense American investment in the Siniora government. Coupled with the situation in Iraq, which had barely improved since the much-touted military surge began, and the persistence of Hamas in Gaza, this alarming development confirmed the degree to which American intervention in the region had worsened Israel's security. Sandwiched now between one Iranian-supported state in the south—however small—and two in the north, Israel was actually much worse off at the end of Bush's final term in office than it was on 9/11. No wonder Israelis were eager for the kind of dramatic security guarantees that the American president offered, and no wonder they wanted to hear them specifically from Bush. Even the Israeli Right had to acknowledge that such declarations were the least that the United States could do. Given how poorly the Israel Defense Forces had performed in recent years, the need for American reassurance of the sort that the president provided was great indeed.

How ironic, then, that Bush's strong words of support were as much for domestic consumption as they were for Israelis. The curious state of affairs in which support for Israel has come to play a role in American politics disproportionate to Americans' actual interest in the country had never been so starkly evident. In other words, stating one's steadfast commitment to Israel has become a political reflex that has less to do with the Middle East than with the U.S. When Barack Obama went through those same motions two months later, the cynicism of the gesture was no less evident.

Following Bush's address, *Ha'aretz* published an editorial suggesting that the president's real intent was to use the tensions between Israel and Iran to maintain control over American policy in the Middle East after his term was over. If Bush could force his successor to continue down the pathway toward a decisive encounter with Iran, then he could win the White House for his agenda regardless of who became the next president. Yet conflating Israeli security requirements with such a long-term strategy for dealing with Iran could only serve to compromise Israel's overall interests further—not just because recent precedent suggests that the U.S. would lose a ground war with the Iranians—potentially implicating those interests in an attempt to affect the results of the American electoral process.

Given the risk that Israel took in inviting a possible conflict with Iran through its campaign in Gaza, it could not prevent critics from speculating that if Israel couldn't get a Republican administration to work with, it might as well try and box the new Democratic administration in so that it would be forced into conducting a similar Middle East policy. Unfortunately, such speculation had the support of loose-lipped Republicans, who were all too eager to promote the possibility of an Israeli conspiracy against Barack Obama. As one senior Bush administration official told the *Washington Post*, Israel's real motivation was to create "facts on the ground" before the new U.S. government took office on January 20.

If this kind of realpolitik doesn't leave a foul taste in your mouth, it most certainly should. Some friend of Israel this official is, confirming that the country's actions were designed to force the next U.S. administration's hand. At the very least, it should inspire observers of Israeli-American relations to understand the depth to which America's conduct in the Middle East during the Bush era brought out the absolute worst in Israeli foreign policy, to an extent that Israel would even consider initiating actions with such potential significance. This kind of behavior cannot be simply reduced to an Israeli desire to direct the foreign policy of the United States for its own ends, even if it runs counter to American interests. Revisiting the dramatic upheaval in the Middle East created by the U.S. in Afghanistan and Iraq during the Bush administration, and how it helped lead to the second Lebanon war, is the only way to understand the "American imprimatur" on Israel's war in Gaza.

ISRAEL AS PROXY

To fully grasp just how detrimental the Bush administration was for Israel, we must look beyond overt American intervention in the Middle East to areas where its influence was more subtly felt. The second Lebanon war, in 2006, is a perfect example. Responding to a cross-border attack in which eight Israeli troops were killed and two more were taken prisoner, Israel decided that it was time to destroy the Shia militia organization Hezbollah once and for all. After Israel conducted massive air and naval bombardments of the organization's installations and missile sites (only introducing ground forces into southern Lebanon ten days after its air offensive began), Hezbollah responded by firing thousands of missiles at northern and central Israel. By the end of the second week in August, a million Lebanese civilians were refugees, 954 were dead, and 3,600 were reported wounded. On the Israeli side, 161 combined military and civilian deaths and 1,750 wounded had been reported, and hundreds of residential homes and buildings had been damaged. According to news reports, almost half of the country's northern population fled southward, with estimates of displaced Israelis rising from 350,000 to as high as 500,000.

The most notable military aspect of this war was its unprecedented brutality. For the first time in the history of the Arab-Israeli conflict, a conventional war was directly waged on each side's civilian populations. Instead of just targeting Israeli military forces, Hezbollah's gunners fired rockets and missiles at dense urban areas. Instead of assaulting military installations, Israeli fighter-bombers and artillery aimed their fire at apartment buildings, houses, bridges, cars, and telecommunications hubs. Hezbollah offered no rationale for delivering their payloads onto civilian targets other than that they were acting in self-defense. Israel conversely explained that it was impossible not to cause civilian casualties because Hezbollah had dispersed its infrastructure and weaponry in urban areas and villages throughout the country. Nevertheless, the IDF and Hezbollah appeared to be operating according to the same set of principles. Functionally, everything was fair game.

Why did both parties choose to risk such a conflict at that point in time? Their mutual willingness to offer up their respective civilian populations to such dire risk meant that both Israel and Hezbollah saw much higher stakes at play than one would expect from a border skirmish. Israeli officials were unmistakably conducting the campaign against Hezbollah as part of a much larger regional struggle. Israel pointed to evidence that the weaponry the Shia militia was using was supplied and manufactured by both Syria and Iran and, in certain instances, operated by Iranian personnel. Israeli politicians and journalists began to piece together the picture of a war initiated by Tehran through Hezbollah, and fought on behalf of its interests, with Syria playing the role of facilitator. Israel was not fighting just to weaken Hezbollah, but as part of a new regional struggle that would pit a global jihad against Western liberal interests.

Or so the story went. But whose story was it? The fact that it was remarkably consistent with the Bush administration's narrative about its own intervention in the Middle East suggested at the very least that Israel and the U.S. had coauthored the script. Factor in Israel's historical tendency to refrain from grouping different conflicts together under one rubric, and it becomes apparent that it was fighting a vicious war at least partly on behalf of its U.S. patron. For the first time in the country's history, Israel found itself in the position of being attacked as an American surrogate by Islamic guerrilla organization acting at least in part on behalf of the interests of a foreign power.

While comparable scenarios have played themselves out during Israel's conflicts with its hostile neighbors— first the U.S. versus the Soviet Union, now the U.S. versus Iran—the use of Middle Eastern countries in a game of strategic chess played by third-party states had never been so utterly transparent. Why? Because as the costs suffered in the second Lebanon war so clearly show, neither Israel nor Hezbollah had anything to gain by going to war. And Lebanon, caught in the middle once again, suffered far greater losses than either of the two belligerents. Only the United States and Iran stood to benefit.

For neoconservatives in the West agitating for an American-led confrontation with Iran, the war in Lebanon was part of a larger strategy. Tehran had finally shown its hand and was actively engaged in the destabilization of the entire region, far beyond the confines of Iraq. Using fundamentalist Lebanese guerrillas as a proxy, it had finally opened up the front against Israel that it had been threatening ever since Ahmadinejad became president in June 2005. And Israel, the United States' most loyal ally, had risen to the occasion.

But the greatest irony of this conflict is how powerless it made the United States look during its fifth year of military engagement in the region. Unable to contain Iran's ambitions of regional hegemony and incapable of quelling a civil war caused by its own invasion of Iraq, America decided to entrust Israel with the responsibility of restoring its lost power of deterrence in the Middle East.

THE EXPLOSION

Avigdor Lieberman's ascension was preordained, or so it seems. There was nothing that Tzipi Livni, the statistical winner of the 2009 Israeli elections, could do to stem his rise, despite her incumbent Kadima Party ("Forward") receiving the most votes. Similarly, while the Likud Party finished second and produced the next government's prime minister, Benjamin Netanyahu, it remained impossible to deny Lieberman's ultimate victory. Indeed, Avigdor Lieberman, the head of Yisrael Beiteinu, the country's fastest-growing party, was increasingly seen to be the next kingmaker in Israeli politics.

With Yisrael Beiteinu eclipsing the Labor Party for the third-largest representation in the Knesset, Lieberman— a former nightclub bouncer from Moldova—seemed bound for greater power and influence. Running on a simple platform of anti-Arab sentiment while using the concept of "loyalty to the state" as his campaign's primary slogan, Lieberman succeeded in making an avowedly racist Jewish political party the ideological winner of a national election.

Though this might seem like a logical result to Israel's critics, it signifies the extent to which the country's political environment has come full circle over the course of the past two decades. In 1994, Israel's parliament went so far as to ban Yisrael Beiteinu's predecessor, the racist Kach Party, following the murder of twenty-nine Palestinians in Hebron by one of its members, Baruch Goldstein. The fact that a political party espousing a similar platform would now be vying for the country's leadership is proof of this transformation. Even worse, no single political party can form a government without its support.

For advocates of peace between Israel and the Palestinians, Lieberman's electoral success leaves no room for optimism. Not just about Israel and Palestine, but also about the Jewish state and its Arab citizenry, which makes up 20 percent of the population. Advocating that those Arabs who do not declare unequivocal loyalty to the state be deprived of their civil rights, offering to "trade" Arab communities inside Israel for settlements in the West Bank, and proposing legislation making it illegal for Israeli Arabs to observe a day of mourning every May 15 (the date the Jewish state was founded), Israel's new foreign minister simultaneously promoted civil conflict between Israelis, and reassured Jewish residents of the Occupied Territories that their settlements will be safe under his watch.

The factors contributing to Yisrael Beiteinu's unlikely popularity are varied. Foremost, the success of the Israeli Right reveals that the conservatives are simply better organized than their liberal counterparts. They project clearer, more defined political messages; they are better at identifying Israeli social grievances, and more adept at cooperating with one another across party lines due to a combination of political discipline and ideological affinity.

At the same time, even though polls indicate that half the country favors a two-state solution and could provide center-left parties with nearly enough votes to govern, there is no leadership in those parties to shep-

herd such a coalition. Thus, for example, though Kadima could forge an alliance with the smaller Labor and
Meretz parties, it would also have to partner with the
Sephardic ultraorthodox Shas Party, and the country's
three Arab-led parties, Balad, Ra'am-Taal, and Hadash.
Predictably, Kadima's reluctance to collaborate with
religious and non-Jewish ethnic parties precludes any
possibility of cross-party cooperation.

Similarly, Kadima's leadership seems to lack awareness of how dramatically it has misruled the country
since it was first elected to power in April 2006. Plagued
by every manner of potential social crisis—a shrinking
public sector, a deteriorating educational system, a dis-
proportionately high rate of child poverty (even though
Israel's economy remained relatively stable under Ehud
Olmert's leadership)—Kadima did nothing to halt the
ongoing erosion of Israeli civil society.

The rise of stereotypically fascist politicians like
Avigdor Lieberman, and his equally toxic ideology, are
natural consequences of their time and place. Lieberman's triumph at precisely the time when Israel's best
friend, the United States, had moved in the opposite political direction, and would soon be offering Israel the
best prospects for an agreeable two-state solution to
date, underlines the extent of this tragedy. By the time
of Barack Obama's first meeting with Netanyahu in May
2009, Israel's new government was steadfastly resisting
the peace process, thereby alienating the Jewish state's
primary friend and patron of forty-plus years.

In fact, the atmosphere surrounding the Obama-
Netanyahu meeting in Washington was nothing short
of poisonous. With Israeli officials leaking a continuous

stream of statements underscoring their apprehension and suspicion of Obama's Middle East policy, and the United States in turn consistently reiterating Israel's obligations to securing a two-state solution, it quickly became clear the meeting was doomed to failure. But most notable was the skepticism and contempt being delivered by the Israeli side.

While members of Israel's ruling coalition would have undoubtedly rationalized their behavior in terms of an evolving set of political differences between the two countries—including the new "leftist, pro-Arab position on the part of the Americans," as a retired Israeli general put it to me two weeks before the meeting—the heart of the problem rested with the new government in Jerusalem. The fact that Israel would consider risking its historical bond with the U.S. in order to dodge its commitment to the peace process revealed the gravity of the situation. That the U.S. government expected such faithful compliance from the new Israeli government is equally distressing.

This is not to say that a Kadima-led government would have necessarily been any better. After all, it was under Kadima's troubled leadership that Israel undertook two highly problematic wars against its neighbors in Gaza and Lebanon—with full U.S. support. Israel's decision to conduct these two campaigns, much like the 1973 Yom Kippur War, helped usher in a new era of conservative hegemony in Israeli politics.

But there has been a remarkable lack of analysis linking the crisis that overtook Israeli-American relations in early 2009 with the political fallout from Israel's recent wars. Nor has much attention been paid to the role of these relations in paving the way for what is inarguably the most reactionary government in Israeli history.

100% DYNAMITE

Since the end of the second Lebanon war, analyses of the conflict have mostly centered on Israel's military failings, facilitated by uncharacteristically poor senior leadership within the country's political and defense echelons. Focused almost entirely on the actions of Prime Minister Olmert, former Chief of Staff Dan Halutz, and former Minister of Defense Amir Peretz, these reports—that an air force general shouldn't have been chief of staff of the armed forces, that a left-wing civilian with no military background shouldn't have been running the Defense Ministry—tend to say more about the ideological concerns of their authors than anything else. This tedious hashing out of the government's failure to manage the war successfully conceals the toll it took on Israeli society. Specifically, it prevents us from seeing who the war's biggest political casualties actually were.

While many pundits have argued that the biggest loser in this conflict was really the United States, which had urged Israel to wage the war as the prelude to a conflict with Iran, the principal political casualty was Israel's parliamentary Left. Led by the example of Defense Minister Peretz and several Labor Party cabinet members who had all done time in Israel's peace movement, many progressives threw their weight behind the war effort. From legendary peacenik and Meretz leader Yossi Beilin telling the *San Francisco Chronicle* that the "operation was very much justified" to internationally acclaimed novelists David Grossman, Amos Oz, and A.B. Yehoshua issuing a joint proclamation supporting the government's prosecution of the engagement, it appeared as though an entire generation of Israeli progressives had crossed over to the other side, and for the first time were using their liberal credibility to sanction an utterly pointless and transparent war.

Having suffered through nearly six years of intermittently intense fighting with Palestinians, and the negative economic growth that this seemed to foster, Israel undeniably needed an ideological break with the government policies that had led it into such an untenable situation. A nation can't prosper—politically or economically—with the kind of polarization Israel experienced in the years leading up to the second Lebanon war.

Describing himself as a "social general" who recognized these heartbreaking quandaries and had concrete proposals to deal with them, Peretz had launched a candidacy for prime minister that appeared to offer Israeli politics something truly different. Campaigning on a peace and social justice platform so resolutely socialist that his desire to become head of Israel's Labor Party appeared doomed from the start, Peretz garnered enough support in the 2005 primaries to shock Labor's Ashkenazi-dominated, ex-general ridden, business-friendly leadership.

Because Peretz's platform promised everything from minimum-wage hikes and the renewal of welfare-state policies, to a bridging of the ethnic divide between Middle Eastern and European Jews and a negotiated settlement with the Palestinians, his victory truly merited the special attention it received from the Israeli press. In the days following his November 9, 2005, triumph over Shimon Peres in Israel's Labor Party leadership primary, *Ha'aretz*, *Yedioth Ahronoth*, and even the *Jerusalem Post* were awash in praise for the fifty-two-year-old Moroccan-born leftist's elevation to the head of Israel's second-largest political party.

Peretz's ascendance was called a "new dawn" and a "rebirth of Israeli democracy," and was branded the most significant event in Israeli politics since the 1977 elections that swept Menachem Begin's Likud Party into power. The consensus was unanimous: for the first time in over a generation, Israelis could distinguish between Right and Left again—or maybe even between right and wrong. Indeed, it would not be far-fetched to compare the reception initially accorded to Peretz to the aspirations many Americans had invested in Barack Obama during the 2008 presidential campaign. Like the former Illinois senator, Peretz was perceived to be the harbinger of a new Israeli social order.

The most interesting aspect of Labor's successful new social platform was how it fit with the West's wider ideological struggles. Labor's critique of Israel's program of privatization, divestment from its public sector, and emphasis on market-based solutions to social problems bore strong affinities to the antiglobalization ideology that had developed over the previous decade. The new Labor Party showed a truly surprising ability to translate these ideas into a mainstream political platform in contemporary Israel, a highly industrialized developed nation undergoing the same economic transformations—from manufacturing to high tech—that the U.S. had been experiencing since the late 1970s.

Though Labor's platform was by no means unique among progressive political parties in the West (consider the French Left's criticisms of neoliberalism, which contributed to that country's rejection of the European Union constitution in 2005), it set itself apart by virtue of its geographical displacement. Although it is in many respects a Western nation, Israel remains a Middle Eastern one as well, plagued by many of the same conflicts that afflict neighboring states, from the role of religion in public life, to the disproportionate influence of the military on civil institutions, to the concentration of the country's wealth in the hands of a dwindling elite class. By successfully promoting a Western social platform in an Israeli context, Labor proved that the global Left's struggle against neoliberalism could be reinvented in the Hebrew vernacular. Or so it seemed in the euphoric days that followed Peretz's defeat of Shimon Peres.

The media of the developed world—whether in Israel, the United States, or Europe—pays an inordinate amount of attention to innovations that come from the Right and Left, often neglecting the center as a consequence. The center doesn't sell, but it also happens to be where most of the political action—as opposed to talk—takes place. Whether you're Ronald Reagan or Amir Peretz, the only way to push a program of change is to win the support, however grudging, of politicians and bureaucrats who benefit from the status quo. The sure sign of a democracy, however flawed, is when its ideologues are forced to move toward the center when they win real power. So the understandable excitement of Peretz's rise in the Labor Party should have been tempered by the impulse to explore what was happening elsewhere. More specifically, the concomitant transformation of the Israeli Right needed to be analyzed more carefully.

Beginning with the August 2005 withdrawal from Gaza orchestrated by Ariel Sharon, every element of the country's post-1960s social order had started to come unraveled. Under the leadership of that Likud Party founder, a new centrist party called Kadima had emerged, recruiting moderate members of both major parties in an attempt to fashion a critical mass with the will to further withdraw from the Occupied Territories. Meanwhile, polls indicated that support for right-wing parties, whether religious or secular, and particularly those focused on a single cause or constituency, appeared to be seriously declining. Was Israel undergoing the sort of progressive transformation that the United States experienced in the 1960s?

Members of the Israeli Left certainly hoped so. Some went so far as to regard Kadima as a stopgap measure, a way for the moderate establishment to forge its place in the new order that would arrive after Labor had become the nation's dominant political force. Others were more circumspect, noting that Sharon and his backers were unlikely to give up power without a protracted struggle. Either way, it seemed certain that major changes were underway. By the time Israel held new parliamentary elections at the end of March 2006, enough of what the Israeli media had identified as a new ideological sensibility during the preceding months made its presence felt at the polls. Although voter turnout was the lowest in Israel's history—suggesting that many had become disenchanted with the political process itself—those who did vote directed most of their animosity at the old order. Kadima had received a predictably large mandate, Labor had come in second, and a brand-new party led by a former Mossad official and representing the social needs of the elderly—the appropriately named Pensioners' Party—had entered parliament.

By contrast, Sharon's former Likud Party had been reduced to a shadow of its former self, and those parties representing the special interests of Israel's religious and settler communities had seemingly done nothing to advance their causes. Though Labor's showing was not as strong as many on the Left had hoped, the outcome of the election still seemed to confirm the optimism inspired by Peretz's rise. After a decade of nearly continuous right-wing rule, Israelis had overwhelmingly demonstrated favor for further withdrawals from the Occupied Territories and openness to government efforts to confront systemic social inequality. Israel appeared to be entering a period of liberalization.

But what exactly did "liberalization" signify in this context? It depended on whom you listened to. To Kadima supporters, it simply meant a growing public acknowledgment that Israel couldn't remain a democratic and Jewish state while maintaining colonial rule over four million Palestinians in the West Bank and Gaza. To proponents of the new Labor Party, the results indicated that Israelis had responded well to its social message. If Kadima managed to stick to its program of withdrawals, it might just develop a real political ideology and become what many Israeli fiscal conservatives hoped it could one day be: a fully Americanized, neoliberal replacement for Likud. And if Labor played its cards right and succeeded in implementing its promised economic reforms under the auspices of a Kadima-led coalition government, it could have a serious chance to become the nation's single political party and turn the country into the Middle East's first social democracy. As it turned out, most of these hopes were dashed within a year.

The first signs of trouble came during the negotiations to form a government with the new Kadima Party. Refused control of the Finance Ministry because of concern that his economic program was too radical, Peretz consented—to the dismay of many of his supporters—to take the unlikely portfolio of defense minister instead. At the time, many political observers argued that this was a sign that Peretz's newly revived Labor Party wouldn't hold the kind of policy sway it had hoped for in the new government. Since Peretz had no military background, argued the more pessimistic commentators, the only reason to make him defense minister must have been to prevent Labor from realizing its social program. As though to confirm this, on the eve of the newly elected government's first day in office, Ehud Olmert signed into law an increase in the price of bread.

Sadly, even the pessimists seemed excessively sanguine about the fate of Labor in the new government. Not only did the party fail to deliver on most of its campaign promises, its new leader and apparent savior went on to squander all the political capital he'd earned over his years in politics on a war that could only be lost. This had a devastating impact on the Israeli Left's future parliamentary prospects. It may even prove to have been worse than Ehud Barak's failure to conclude a final status agreement with the Palestinians in 2000, the event that led to the outbreak of the second intifada. The gains made by Avigdor Lieberman in the 2009 elections do little to dampen this suspicion.

In discussing the consequences of the second Lebanon war, many analysts have pointed out that it ended Ehud Olmert's plan to make more unilateral withdrawals from the West Bank. Instead of picking up where Sharon left off after suffering a stroke, Olmert found himself stymied by the time he announced his resignation in July 2008, with only a tenuous cease-fire with Hamas to show for his peacemaking efforts. But focusing on that turn of events conceals how the war affected the Left. Despite scandals and general unhappiness with his leadership throughout Israeli society, Olmert was still there to greet Bush at the Knesset and shun Jimmy Carter the month before. Peretz, on the other hand, had gone from being one of the brightest stars in the sky to a dark patch at its furthest reaches. It was Labor that ended up feeling the greatest fallout from the military's failure to deal Hezbollah a decisive blow or, more importantly, protect Israeli citizens from harm.

In the weeks immediately after the end of the second Lebanon war, Israel's four-month-old government appeared to be in free fall. Opposition politicians demanded the resignation of the prime minister, the defense minister, and the military chief of staff for their handling of the conflict. Reservists protested having been sent out to battle without proper equipment, training, or operational plans. Senior officials from the prime minister to the president and the justice minister

were under investigation for everything from engaging
in illegal real-estate transactions to sexual harassment.
Thousands of civilians made homeless by Hezbollah
rocket fire were demanding government assistance. And
in February 2008, the National Insurance Institute published its biannual state poverty report: 24.7 percent of
Israel's population was living below the poverty line, a
third of them children.

For most Israelis, everything that took place after
the war amounted to business as usual, the very state
of affairs that had presumably suppressed voter turnout
in the first place. Yet it required markedly more effort
to maintain the status quo, and the toll on Israel's resources became more and more evident. The problems
Israel now faced typified a slow but sure crisis that had
begun in earnest during the Sharon years, if not during the two governments prior to his led by Ehud Barak
and Benjamin Netanyahu. Instead of that break with the
recent past for which so many Israelis had been yearning in the period leading up to the 2006 elections, they
found themselves with more of the same—only at a
higher cost.

THE GREECE OF THE MIDDLE EAST

For those who see the Middle East as a real-world analogy for the fate of Sisyphus—the mythological figure
who was forever doomed to repeat the same work over
and over again—the fortieth anniversary of the June 1967
Six-Day War left little room for hope. During a month's
worth of commemorations in the Israeli media, public
conferences, lectures, and tours of the West Bank led
by left-wing NGOs like Peace Now, it didn't just seem

as if little had changed for the better over the last four decades—on the eve of the second Lebanon war's first anniversary, little had improved over the previous year.

The military situation in the south remained as dire as when the government had been elected the previous March. At times subject to up to forty missile attacks a day, the 20,000 residents of the town of Sderot (which lies a kilometer from the Gaza Strip) had all but emptied out. This suggested to some analysts a complete rout of the Israel Defense Forces, which once had a reputation that would have made such a turn of events seem impossible. Resembling the previous summer's near-evacuation of the north due to the IDF's inability to stem the delivery of small-caliber rocket fire across the Lebanese border, events in Sderot indicated to many military officials and journalists that Hamas and Islamic Jihad had achieved the same level of strategic importance as Hezbollah.

Without a diplomatic solution to the crisis in the south and unable to prevent the launching of rockets by military means, Israel had placed its bets on Palestinian President Mahmoud Abbas's Fatah Party reestablishing military control over Gaza. In May 2007, the escalation of fire against Israel coincided with a Hamas initiative to prevent Fatah from taking power. After months of intermittent fighting, which stoked a growing concern that Palestinians were on the verge of a civil war, forces loyal to the Hamas-led government of Ismail Haniyeh took full control of the territory in early June, either killing, imprisoning, or sending abroad those remaining Fatah forces that did not accept its right to rule.

For the first time in the history of the Arab-Israeli

conflict, a Palestinian government ruled over a part of historic Palestine without any Israeli cooperation. Granted, Israeli utility companies still supplied the strip with power, water, fuel, and telephone service, and Israeli forces continued to control Gaza's physical borders. Yet, both politically and military, Hamas had achieved genuine independence as a result of a struggle against Israel and its allied Palestinian forces.

It was a major coup: an organization that had controlled the Palestinian Authority's government for a year and a half without once recognizing Israel, despite enormous international pressure to do so, was now running its own independent canton. If it meant losing both American and European economic aid in the process, that was a sacrifice Hamas was willing to make. Things were already so bad in Gaza—one of the poorest places on the globe—that Hamas could afford to put political goals ahead of economic necessity. When you have nothing, it's hard to get riled up about how that nothing is divided up. At least, that seemed to be what Hamas' leadership had concluded.

At first, the meaning of Hamas' success was obscured by the fact that its victory had formally severed Gaza from the West Bank and thus cut Palestine in half. Eager to take advantage of this situation and how it might result in a more friendly, Fatah-led Palestinian state in the West Bank, both Israel and the United States, along with their Arab allies, moved quickly to bestow national legitimacy on President Abbas and his governmental apparatus in Ramallah. Hundreds of millions of dollars in tax money and aid withheld since Hamas' 2006 election were released to Abbas, together with military and diplomatic recognition. The severe limits of Fatah's power didn't matter as long as Palestinians could see how much better they might fare internationally if they rejected Hamas.

But in June 2007, at a hastily convened international summit in the Egyptian resort of Sharm el-Sheikh that saw Abbas meet with Israeli, Jordanian, and Egyptian leaders, reality finally set in. The overall mood was grim. All the leaders in attendance spoke cautiously about how to handle Hamas, and made it clear that they appreciated both the significance of the group's victory and the threat it might pose to regional stability.

A successful Islamic regime in Gaza spelled trouble for the Egyptian government, which for years has struggled against its own Sunni militants, including Hamas' parent organization, the Muslim Brotherhood. With its own Sunnis radicalized by the situation in Iraq, and the region's largest Palestinian refugee population, the Jordanian monarchy faced similarly difficult prospects in managing the fallout. And Abbas, though undoubtedly stronger in the West Bank than in Gaza, was by no means assured of his own stability despite the foreign assistance that Fatah received. After all, his forces had just been defeated in spite of strong backing by the United States, Western Europe, Israel, and leading Arab states. If you can't win with that sort of support, you must be very weak indeed.

All this explains why, despite pro forma statements of outrage at the death and destruction the IDF caused during its incursion into Gaza at the end of 2008, neither the Egyptian government nor the Palestinian president took measures to back up their criticisms of the

Israeli operation. Mahmoud Abbas's response was sufficiently underwhelming to give Hamas the ammunition it needed to declare that Fatah had helped the IDF plan and conduct the operation in Gaza. The executions and maimings that followed the cease-fire testified, as Hamas sought to punish "traitors," to the degree of its isolation not only from the West, but also from its Arab neighbors.

Iran, however, was a significant exception. Many experts suspected that Hamas was receiving the same sort of aid from Iran that Hezbollah enjoyed, despite the fact that it was a Sunni organization. For the Arab states that had attended the Sharm el-Sheikh summit and Israel alike, the biggest nightmare scenario created by the Hamas victory was the specter of an Iranian outpost being established on Israel's southern border. Combined with fresh and, according to the United Nations, recently rearmed Hezbollah forces facing Israel to the north, such a puppet state in Gaza would give Iran the previously unimaginable ability to wage a multifront campaign against the Jewish state that wouldn't require the use of air power or conventional ground forces to achieve significant results. Even more frightening still was what this implied about Israel's inability to contain such threats: in military terms, the country's deterrent power was continuing to decline.

On the political front, other than the replacement of Defense Minister Peretz by former Prime Minister Barak, the dismissal of Finance Minister Avraham Hirschon from Kadima for corruption, and the addition of Yisrael Beiteinu Chairman Avigdor Lieberman to the newly designated minister of strategic affairs cabinet portfolio,

no additional ministerial positions changed as a consequence of 2006's conflict with Hezbollah. Despite some
of the worst poll ratings in Israeli history and the half-
release of the first official report (supervised by retired
judge Eliyahu Winograd) documenting the government's
wartime failings, Ehud Olmert's coalition remained in
power.

This government had every reason to fall. It appeared impervious to concerns about what had just
transpired in Gaza. The public was pessimistic that new
elections could change anything about the country's
economic or security situation. A parliamentary effort
to keep the Kadima-Labor coalition in power succeeded
only because a Likud-led government under the leadership of opposition chief Benjamin Netanyahu actually
seemed—at least for a short while—to be worse. So a
year after the Lebanon war, the government showed no
signs of going down.

In a way, the situation was similar to the one in the
U.S., where the abject failure of the Bush administration's imperial program didn't affect its hold on the
day-to-day operations of the government, even after the
November 2006 elections had returned the Democratic
Party to power in Congress. Against all odds, the Olmert
government appeared to be one of the more stable in
recent Israeli history.

On the fortieth anniversary of the Six-Day War, the
only issues driving Israelis into the streets were related
to gender: the right to hold a gay pride parade in Jerusalem, and the Justice Ministry's handling of the sexual
indiscretions on the part of the country's recently "retired" president, Moshe Katsav. Though the minimum

wage had partially risen over the course of the previous year (to half the amount that the government had initially promised) and the economy had made a mild recovery from the war, public commemoration of the 1967 conflict's anniversary ironically displaced any explicit discussion of what had transpired over the previous year.

There was no debate in the public sphere about the social issues that the Labor Party had championed in the wake of the disengagement two years before, not to mention the cultural issues raised by the ethnic identity of its onetime Mizrahi leader Amir Peretz. Led again by Ehud Barak—now, tellingly, a millionaire after six years out of politics—Labor was largely indistinguishable from Kadima. Security was again at the top of its agenda. And Israel's special relationship with the U.S. was as strong as ever, despite all the problems it had caused in recent years.

Israeli intellectuals on both the Left and Right expressed resentment of the United States (much like the sort demonstrated by their European counterparts), and there was a growing desire of many domestic political figures to become closer to the European Union. Even so, Israeli dependence on the Bush administration for cues on how and when to act remained unexamined.

The political landscape throughout the Middle East and adjoining portions of West Asia had so profoundly deteriorated that few Israelis believed they could afford to fully redirect American policy in the region. Fear discouraged a critique when it was most necessary. Again, the analogy to the domestic situation in the United States is apt. Just as liberal Democrats went along with everything from the Patriot Act in 2001 through to the reauthorization of FISA in 2008, Israelis of all political persuasions felt compelled to toe the line in support of the Bush Doctrine, despite their private misgivings.

Keeping It Real

Perhaps Israelis and Americans were both playing out a waiting game. So long as the Bush administration was in power, any progress seemed unlikely outside of the parameters established by American military engagement in the region. This may be why the president's May 2008 trip to Israel inspired such a predictable response. The only lively goings-on concerned the American presidential contest and its implications for the special relationship.

Whether the damage wrought by the Bush era can ever be undone remains to be seen. But it's still worth pondering the alternatives to the special relationship. During that period, Israeli progressives increasingly looked to Europe for the ideological and financial support they weren't getting from the United States. Though liberal Jewish American organizations like the New Israel Fund made significant efforts to redress this deficit (with numerous philanthropically funded social assistance, worker training, and educational programs) and new policy-oriented fronts like J Street had arisen to challenge the influence of AIPAC, the perception remained that when it comes to Israel, Europeans still hold a monopoly on progressivism.

Witness the coverage given to Israel-boycott initiatives by British university instructors. Whereas the British press sometimes identifies the U.S. with Christian Zionists who love Israel to theological death, many American and Israeli periodicals see the UK as the home of a growing anti-Semitic Left that's eager to do things like punish Israeli educators to protest Israel's treatment of the Palestinians. This makes the increasing intimacy between Israel and the European Union that has developed over the 2000s all the more fascinating. Even though the large-scale deployment of European peacekeeping forces in Lebanon after the war in 2006 was a reminder of Israel's failures—underscored by the international condemnation of their treatment of civilians—those troops still managed to inspire questions about what the region might look like with a long-term financial and political presence by the EU. In fact, it made some older Israelis—who had lived through decades of the special relationship with the U.S.—nostalgic for a time when France and Israel were more closely allied.

One of this book's main purposes is to articulate my discomfort about what the special relationship between the U.S. and Israel has become. As both an American and an Israeli, I'm deeply invested in this relationship. On a personal level, it speaks to my own desire to reconcile the geographic divisions that have complicated the history of my family and made me feel at times both literally and figuratively cut in half. But sometimes partnerships reach a point where they must come to an end for the good of both parties. While others must submit to counseling, lest they risk meeting that sad fate. At the very least, Israel and the United States need to reconsider their relations. Commitment without questions, in spite of all the ensuing pain, will be disastrous for Israelis; to a degree, it already has been. And it can become almost as damaging for Americans, as suggested by the worrisome prognostications of academics John Mearsheimer and Stephen Walt on the role of the Israel lobby in American politics.

I share this conviction with a great many Americans and Israelis, Jews and Gentiles. Many want to see some kind of distance between the two countries, both strategically and diplomatically. Examples abound of the destructive aspects of the special relationship. Americans have been responsible (whether by direct export or dubious example) for some of Israel's worst religious and economic problems, such as the stereotypical American fundamentalist settler—think Baruch Goldstein, the perpetrator of the 1994 Hebron massacre, or Rabbi Meir Kahane—and the profoundly enthusiastic embrace of a technology-driven neoliberalism by Israel's business community.

Yet it is possible for new blood from the Diaspora to bring its energy to Israel without promoting an us-versus-them mentality that makes pragmatic compromises difficult. It's also possible for the entrepreneurial spirit to create more jobs without dismantling what remains of Israel's welfare state and its historically vital public sector. Indeed, this is where the growing influence of Europe looms largest. Despite its own history of struggling to accommodate ethnic difference and immigration, the European Union can provide an example for Israel that's different from that of the U.S., particularly on issues of social and economic justice.

Americans need to travel abroad, particularly to places like Israel that are heavily covered in the international media, in order to be reminded that what they read on their computer screens or see on TV is only part of the story. Precisely because Israel is so frequently in the news, many Americans assume that the country is identical with what they see on their screens. But that presumption is as wrong as the one that led many international commentators to wonder why all Americans were marching in lockstep to the beat of George W. Bush's drum in the months leading up to the Iraq War. Even in the immediate aftermath of 9/11, when Americans united in a way unprecedented since World War II, plenty of people were willing to state their belief that the Bush administration wasn't going to act in the nation's best interest. But you'd never have believed it had you gotten all of your information from the mainstream media.

The U.S. has so thoroughly destabilized the balance of power in the Middle East that any peace agreement Israel does end up signing with the Palestinians might turn out to do little to promote actual peace. Muslims throughout the region are so angry at what has transpired since the start of the Iraq War that concessions to the Palestinian people will not be enough to placate them. In a sense, the power to act purposefully is no longer in Israel's hands. Critically neglected, this concern appears to be hovering on the horizon for many Middle Eastern analysts as debates rage about whether the United States and Israel ought to engage Iran militarily, or whether al-Qaeda will replace Palestinian organizations such as Hamas and Islamic Jihad if and when Israel is able to neutralize them.

If general peace in the region depends on a resolution to the Palestinian-Israeli conflict, it's precisely because the conflict has now transcended the physical borders of both Israel and Palestine. In other words, the peace will require the U.S. to make amends throughout the region and then find a way to marginalize the remaining regimes and organizations that refuse to accept an apology. Israel can do little without this sort of hard-nosed diplomacy. But it has to go along with such an approach, even if it means submitting to requests from the United States that in the past would have only served the latter's interests.

CHAPTER SIX

SAFE EUROPEAN HOME

THIS IS ENGLAND

It was as though history had come full circle. Thirty-nine years after the government of Harold Wilson announced it would embargo the delivery of Chieftain tanks to the Israel Defense Forces, a decision that would accelerate Israel's movement away from Europe and into the arms of the United States for the next four decades, Israeli President Shimon Peres found himself being feted by Britain's establishment. Awarded an honorary doctorate by King's College in 2008, invited to address both houses of Parliament, and granted knighthood by the Queen, Israel's best-known Europhile had finally returned home at age eighty-five.

Well, not exactly. Rather, he had found an exceedingly warm welcome in a place that had long embodied rejection for Israelis due to its history of anti-Semitism, the perception of Arab influence over government policy, and anti-Zionist trends among Britain's intellectuals and news media. Despite—or maybe even because of—this apprehension, Israelis had consistently voiced the opinion that the only way to reconcile properly with Europe was to begin with the nation that had been Palestine's colonial master.

Given how strongly both countries had collaborated in matters of security since 9/11, it was probably inevitable that relations would warm between the two governments. Yet it was not until the second Lebanon war, when a large-scale commitment of European peacekeepers to the United Nations Interim Forces in Lebanon (UNIFIL) was made, that one saw the historic distance between Israel and the EU diminish enough to imagine someone like Peres being knighted. With the election of Nicolas Sarkozy to the presidency and his subsequent courtship of Israel, it seemed that it was just a matter of time before France would follow suit.

To liberal Israelis eager to see their country distance itself from the United States in the wake of the Bush administration's disastrous Middle East policies, such interactions inspired hope for a more rational foreign sponsor. Whereas the pretense to balance that has typically characterized European states' relations with Israel might once have been regarded as annoyingly distant, it now seemed like a selling point. The United Kingdom would gladly purchase Israeli military equipment, such as drones and targeting pods, but it would still insist that Israel label products manufactured in the Occupied Territories, and would levy tariffs on such goods. Such complexity has not been part of American policy toward Israel for many years. For example, the U.S. State Department hasn't tied loan guarantees to progress in peace negotiations since the early 1990s.

Yet there was something oddly reassuring about a confrontation the Israeli president had with demonstra-

tors while speaking at Oxford on the same day as his
King's College visit. With high-profile British academics
so outspoken on the subject of the occupation, how
could Peres not have anticipated being denounced by
some members of the audience as a war criminal? The
Olmert government, however much it may have tol-
erated the expansion of settlements during its near
three-year tenure, seemed eager to place the task of
dismantling them on a foreign government's shoulders.
In this way, Israel could better manage the stress of its
own domestic conflicts. Let the British be the bad guy;
let the Americans play the role of enforcer. Such possibilities were not lost on Peres, who suggested in his
address to Parliament that an Israeli civil war was entirely possible in the event of a withdrawal from the
territories.

And so it remains politically expedient for Israel's
ruling class to engage in rhetorical combat with the
European Left—precisely because it deflects attention
away from lingering questions about the settlements.
Export the conflict to Europe and leave it at that. Demonstrating on Israeli television that you have done so
also has its public relations value.

The real question is what value the British government accrued from Peres's visit. It certainly wasn't
staged as a charity event. And its timing cannot be
discounted, particularly since it came in the wake of
the Democratic Party's major victory in the 2008 election and the implicit verdict that this result cast on the
Bush administration's approach to foreign policy. Having spent the last four decades playing second fiddle to
the United States in Middle East affairs, never as promi-

nently as under Tony Blair's residency at 10 Downing Street, the United Kingdom had an ideal opportunity to display some leadership. Because no one had made a bigger show of bringing Israel back to the European fold than French President Sarkozy, however, the British had to compensate for the lateness of their efforts. This is why it made perfect sense that they welcomed President Peres with an overkill of pomp and circumstance.

Emancipation Proclamation

It is hard to break old habits, though. The special relationship between the United States and Israel has been steady for so long that representatives of both nations struggle to see an alternative. Asked whether Israel would agree to a cease-fire plan for Gaza being worked out by Sarkozy, American military analyst Anthony Cordesman was predictably pessimistic. He told the BBC that it did not matter what kind of shuttle diplomacy the Europeans might be engaging in: Israel's military operations in Gaza would only cease when its armed forces had accomplished all of their assigned objectives. Besides, the analyst respectfully chided his interviewer, Israel will only stop if America orders it to do so.

The script was all too familiar. Even though Cordesman was being asked what it would take to halt Israeli operations in Gaza, his reply could have been issued in response to any number of Israeli military campaigns over the last thirty years: in Lebanon, Gaza, or the West Bank during the al-Aksa Intifada. The ritual performances were being played out with the usual efficiency. As Palestinian civilian casualties piled up, European states petitioned Israel to act with restraint. Arab and

EU delegates to the UN worked toward a cease-fire. And the United States continued to shield Israel. It appeared that hope for change in the region had once again been revealed to be a mirage.

But then, in a surprising act, just hours after Cordesman was interviewed by the BBC, Israel agreed to implement a daily three-hour cease-fire in order to allow residents of Gaza to obtain relief supplies delivered through corridors set up by Israeli forces. Though not the full cease-fire sought by Sarkozy, the move certainly reflected the pressure generated by his diplomatic activities, along with intense Israeli embarrassment over the killing of forty people in an IDF attack on a UN school the day before. This was the price Israel would have to pay for the error. Not wanting to be sidelined, the United States also gave its official blessing.

Undertaken during the first week of the Gaza war, the French president's diplomatic initiative received widespread international support. Proposing the deployment of international forces to locate and destroy the smuggling tunnels along the Israel-Egypt border through which Hamas had been bringing its weaponry into the Palestinian territory, together with a French-led naval force to patrol Gaza's coast, Sarkozy's plan echoed the approach taken two years before during the second Lebanon war, in which relief efforts were paired with measures to curtail the flow of arms. This time, however, it seemed more likely to succeed—if Israel could be persuaded to go along with the plan.

Sarkozy's efforts during the Gaza conflict were emblematic of the increasingly forceful European involvement in peacemaking efforts in the Middle East that began during the final years of the Bush administration. France's effort to position itself as an arbitrator between Israel and its Arab neighbors is of particular significance for Israel's political establishment. Diplomatic and military allies until the 1967 Six-Day War, when French President Charles de Gaulle decided to suspend military aid to Israel over its seizure of Arab lands, Israel and France once had their own special relationship.

Under the leadership of Kadima's Ehud Olmert, Israel consistently welcomed Sarkozy's diplomatic outreach, seeing it as an opportunity to edge out from underneath the increasingly problematic American umbrella. And Sarkozy responded in kind, winding up his tenure as the president of the European Union by successfully pushing the organization to significantly upgrade its relationship with Israel to observer status, along with forging closer defense, security, and economic ties.

Nonetheless, despite the generally favorable attitude toward France's intervention in the region conveyed in the global press during the Gaza campaign, many critics of Israeli policy were concerned that European motivation was itself suspect. They worried that instead of being ideologically impelled by a desire to bring about peace in the region, Europe was simply seizing an opportunity to export weaponry and create new commercial ties. Informing these fears was a general sense that Europe had undergone a political transformation during the War on Terror, one which allowed it to take an interest in Israel because its values had been "Americanized."

Hearing German Chancellor Angela Merkel blame the present situation in Gaza "clearly and exclusively" on

Hamas, and Czech Foreign Minister Karel Schwarzen-
berg state that "Hamas has excluded itself from serious
political dialogue," did nothing to soothe these anxieties. Still, there was always the possibility that such ut-
terances were strategic (rather than a direct expression
of European attitudes)—an attempt to reassure anxious
Israeli politicians, who needed to have their new European partners sound more American than the Americans. That certainly seems to have been one function of
the numerous "pro-Israel" statements, such as threatening Iran with military action if it develops nuclear
weaponry, which Sarkozy and French Foreign Minister
Bernard Kouchner have made since assuming office in
May 2007.

Certainly, in matters of Middle East policy, Europe
had inarguably moved to the right during the Bush
years, particularly, as its critics argued, under the influence of rising Islamophobia in the wake of terrorist
actions in Madrid and London in 2004–5. At the very
least, though, the diplomatic achievements of Sarkozy
during Israel's incursion into Gaza came as a relief to a
world weary of the status quo. And they also served as
a reminder that the history of Israel, as well as the rest
of the Middle East, might have been quite different had
France and Great Britain not punished Israel for its actions in the Six-Day War.

RUMORS AND SUSPICIONS

Tangible signs of the thawing in Israeli-European re-
lations had actually begun to appear well before the
Gaza conflict. By the end of the first week of the second
Lebanon war, rumors began to make their way through

Israeli diplomatic and military circles that negotiations with European nations were underway for the expansion of the UNIFIL presence in southern Lebanon. Initiated by Israel's new foreign minister, Tzipi Livni, this move signaled that long-standing Israeli concerns about the effectiveness of United Nations forces in Lebanon—some would say long-standing hostility as well—had dissipated. More to the point, it demonstrated that Israel's Foreign Ministry believed that the military campaign against Hezbollah would not succeed.

Less than a month later, after the UN Security Council adopted Resolution 1701, Livni could safely say that she had achieved her goal. Authorizing UNIFIL to boost its troop numbers to 15,000 from a force of 2,000, and extending its mandate for the first time since its establishment back in 1978 to include the use of force, the resolution also specified the formation of a maritime component intended to halt the smuggling of weapons by sea. Though European troops had consistently taken part in UNIFIL since its formation, this expanded version of the force had a contingent of over 7,000 NATO soldiers, including large brigades from France, Italy, Spain, and Germany.

Boasting of the unprecedented European contribution to this force, a UN press release noted that in previous years, only 6 percent of the organization's global peacekeeping operations had come from European countries. By committing so many troops to this one operation in Lebanon, Europe had doubled its previous level of contribution to UN peacekeeping initiatives. Instructed to create a buffer zone between Israeli and Hezbollah forces and clear southern Lebanon of mines, cluster munitions, and other unexploded ordinance, UNIFIL's increased responsibilities reflected a deepening international commitment to securing peace in the Middle East.

For anyone familiar with the history of Israel's relations with both Europe and the United Nations—particularly the so-called "Zionism Is Racism" UN resolution of 1975—the August 11, 2006, Security Council agreement clearly marked a watershed. The significance of the UN coordinating an international peacekeeping force to help safeguard Israel, over half of which came from Europe, cannot be overemphasized.

From the early 1950s until 1967, Israel had received the bulk of its military assistance from France and, to a smaller extent, other European states such as Belgium and the United Kingdom. The two iconographic weapons that "won" the Six-Day War—the French-manufactured Mirage III fighter-bomber and the British Centurion tank— stand out. Following Israel's decision to attack Egypt, Syria, and Jordan in June 1967, however, France suspended its military cooperation with the country, and defense contracts for its next-generation Mirage V combat aircraft and the United Kingdom's Chieftain battle tank were also canceled. Both countries cited the need to preserve good relations with Arab states as the reason for this abrupt change. From that period until the aftermath of the second Lebanon war, there was no significant military cooperation between Europe and Israel.

While the limitation of Anglo-French defense sales to Israel in the late 1960s did not coincide with a similar decline in trade, the decision still came as a major blow. Having just secured at least temporary dominion over the Sinai Peninsula, the Golan Heights, and the West Bank, Israel's defense requirements were considerably greater than they had been before the Six-Day War. Sometimes success causes as many problems as it solves, especially when it comes as rapidly as it did for Israel in 1967. Despite the newfound confidence, bordering at times on feelings of invincibility that infused Israelis after their decisive triumph, the country was also more vulnerable in some respects than it had been previously. Surely their Arab antagonists were going to mount a massive counterattack to reclaim what the Israelis had taken from them, flush with new weapons. How could Israel respond effectively without the European support it had relied on for the previous two decades?

In the end, that counterattack took long enough to arrive that the depletion of Israeli forces was not an issue. The United States more than adequately compensated for the loss of European military assistance. But the sense of betrayal Israel's leadership felt at the time remained. The perception was that Europe was staying true to its history of anti-Semitism by deserting the Jewish people at their most crucial hour of need. Regardless of how enlightened European motivations for suspending commercial defense relations with Israel actually were—both France and the United Kingdom indeed increased their export sales throughout the Middle East during the 1970s and 1980s—France's decision in particular to impose a fairly wide-ranging arms embargo beginning in 1968 was like salt being rubbed into still-open wounds.

Because of the Holocaust, or so the common wisdom of the time held, Europe was obliged to take extra precautions where Israel was concerned. Israel still had relatively warm relations with West Germany, which provided both military and economic aid without interruption. Yet the only Western European states with large-scale industrial concerns manufacturing military equipment at that time were the two countries which, though they had obviously not impacted Jewish life as negatively as Germany, had the capacity to keep subsidizing the moral debt—and failed to do so. Perhaps that capriciousness was to be expected of the United Kingdom, whose history as a colonial power had complicated its place in the region. But France was different. As the first European state to promote Jewish emancipation—not just within France itself, but in Europe as whole—it made sense to Israelis that the nation would also be amongst the first to secure the Israeli right to be equal among nations.

J'ACCUSE

To say that Israelis felt abandoned by French President Charles de Gaulle's decision to suspend military aid to Israel in the wake of the Jewish state's declaration of war in June 1967 would be a gross understatement. Regarding it as a cultural rejection as much as a diplomatic one, they saw the late French leader personifying everything that was wrong with postwar Europe. Since de Gaulle was considered a stereotypically provincial, self-serving military man, it was assumed that the decision was motivated by personal preference more than political savvy. If he was reorienting France toward the Arab world, the real explanation must be that he had been waiting all along for the proper moment to act on his petite bourgeois anti-Semitism.

De Gaulle's statement that Jews were "elite people, self-confident and dominating" during a November 1967 press conference criticizing Israel's seizure of what would become the Occupied Territories did little to mitigate such suspicions. It was a deplorable and unfortunate remark that ran directly counter to the president's purposes. Because the French leader combined this loaded characterization with the prediction that Israel would only be able to hold on to the territories through "an occupation that cannot but involve oppression, repression, expropriation," and that it would come to describe resistance to its rule as "terrorism," he laid the perfect foundation for conservative arguments that antioccupation discourses are inevitably racist.

The possibility that military and strategic considerations, not to mention France's recent withdrawal from Algeria, might have played a role in de Gaulle's overhaul of French foreign policy in the Middle East either did not occur to most Jews or was dismissed as irrelevant. I remember dining at a cousin's house in Paris in 1977, when Raymond, a French relative of ours and a lifelong Communist Party member, voiced the anger that was still simmering a decade later; he put down his fork rather forcefully and said, "*Vraiment*. De Gaulle sold us out just like the rest of them. They just don't like Jews."

Raymond's anger may have been understandable—he had lost most of his immediate family in concentration camps during the Second World War—but it typified a failure to give de Gaulle his due. As rude, inconsistent, and poorly worded as the original decision to suspend arms sales had been, de Gaulle's about-face was under-

taken after deep reflection on what France had learned
from its disastrous final years in North Africa. He feared,
quite simply, that the Israelis were embarking, perhaps
unwittingly, on the same sort of colonial project France
had just given up in Algeria. In a December 1967 letter
to former Israeli Prime Minister David Ben Gurion, de
Gaulle expressed grave misgivings about Israel's "taking
possession of Jerusalem by armed force, as well as many
Jordanian, Egyptian, and Syrian territories," and then
"practicing the repression and expulsions which are the
inevitable consequence of an occupation that is really
more of an annexation."*

Despite the limitations of de Gaulle's worldview,
laid bare by French students and their supporters in
the following year on the streets of Paris, the benefit
of hindsight makes it hard to take issue with such an
admonition. However patronizing it may have come
across to Israelis at the time, it was plainly the advice of
someone who had personal experience of a brutal colonial war in which the French military had deployed all
manner of counterinsurgency policies against the Alge-
rians and still lost. And de Gaulle's estimations of Israeli
territorial ambitions were fundamentally correct. While
Israel would later withdraw from the Sinai as a consequence of the Camp David Accords, its horrific treatment of the civilian populations in the West Bank and
Gaza ended up matching de Gaulle's description. What
remains open to question, however, is whether the prescience of the French president coincided with a genuine personal hostility toward Jews.

*Translation of de Gaulle's letter excerpted from *Middle Eastern Conflicts*, by
François Massoulié (Interlink Publishing, 1998).

Some with a firm grasp of the historical record insist that it did. But there is also compelling evidence to the contrary. Consider the following: in the same letter to Ben Gurion, de Gaulle went on to express genuine frustration over the situation created by Israel's acquisitions of these new lands. "Israel went beyond the limits of necessary moderation," he wrote. "I regret it all the more since on the condition of your troops' withdrawal, it appears that a solution including the recognition of your State by its neighbors . . . would today be possible within the framework of the United Nations, a solution which France is finally disposed to work toward." In other words, while moving from defense to offense, Israel might have lost the chance to achieve the recognition that had been eluding it. "This outcome would bring peace to the Middle East, facilitate world understanding, and, I think, would serve the interests of the people concerned, including yours. This is how Israel could become a state like any other instead of continually parading its moving two-thousand-year exile." To be sure, the tone of de Gaulle's letter is condescending. But its content speaks to the current situation, over forty years later, with eerie accuracy.

Indeed, this analysis could easily be issued today from the mouth of former Israeli Prime Minister Ehud Olmert or a Diaspora antioccupation activist alike. How might we account for this? Perhaps it is time to revise our understanding of de Gaulle's action. What if the split between Israel and Europe in the wake of the Six-Day War did not represent a reiteration of older forms of hostility toward Jews? What if the concern itself was simply the consequence of a reflex, given that only twenty years had passed since World War II? What if it instead signaled an ideological divergence rooted more in attitudes toward colonialism, for which both France and the United Kingdom were both paying a steep price? What if the Europeans were finally beginning to grasp the realization that the doctrine of "peace through war" was doomed to failure?

Although the immediate result of the French decision to cease arms sales to Israel was to lead the latter to take shelter in the American aegis, that does not necessarily mean that de Gaulle desired such an outcome. Unfortunately, however, the special relationship that developed between the United States and Israel ended up reinforcing the very logic that de Gaulle was arguing against. For the United States of the Vietnam War was assuredly a country bent on promoting peace through war.

If Israelis today lament the break with Europe after the Six-Day War, it is because they are at least partially aware that the path suggested by de Gaulle might have led somewhere better than the one shepherded by the United States. When reflecting on the appeals made by Israelis on both the Right and the Left since the second Lebanon war for Europe to increase its involvement in the region, it is crucial to bear this sense of lost opportunity in mind. The Europe of today is vastly different than it was in 1967 and, for the most part, far more conservative in matters pertaining to the greater Middle East. As exemplified by British and French deployments in Iraq and Afghanistan, Europe has lost some of its previous inhibitions about collaborating with America's Middle East policy. Thus, in retrospect, de Gaulle turns out to seem a lot more "progressive" than anyone might have guessed at the time. Despite his clear fondness for Israel, it is difficult to imagine current President Nicholas Sarkozy expressing himself in the manner that de Gaulle did in his letter to Ben Gurion. The degree of emotion in that missive, its sense of being suffused with real regret instead of the ritualistically performed sort, serves as a potent reminder of what might have been had Israel found a way to change course in 1967.

As far as France is concerned, things are very different today. (In May 2009, France opened its first military base in the Gulf. Located in Abu Dhabi, the installation, dubbed "Peace Camp," is 137 miles from Iran.) Some might say that the country's foreign policy is more nuanced. Others might accuse it of lacking substance. Consider the contrast between Sarkozy telling Algeria's prime minister in the fall of 2007 that the era of colonialism is over, versus his foreign minister, Bernard Kouchner, telling an Israeli audience that same autumn that France would be willing to go to war over Iran's nuclear program. The lack of ideological consistency was obvious, however laudable the intentions. Even Jacques Chirac, the last of the country's towering postwar figures, ended his tenure amid hesitancy and confusion. Although the French voters who elected Sarkozy hoped that he might put an end to his country's meanderings—after all, he had risen to prominence by making forceful statements about the need to ensure law and order within France and to act with conviction, rather than *ressentiment*, on the international stage—many suspected that, at least when it came to the Middle East, he was merely attempting to take over the United States' role in the region in order to assume the obvious economic benefits that come with it.

THE WAY THEY WERE

The French and British decision to limit arms sales to Israel after the Six-Day War went hand in hand with a metamorphosis in the global Left's perspectives on the Middle East. While American leftists showed increasing interest in "third world liberation" as the 1960s wore on, they focused most of their attention on Southeast Asia and, closer to home, the inner city. In Europe, by contrast, the end of colonial rule in Africa and Asia made it possible for leftists to concentrate on a variety of causes around the world. The Vietnam War was a topic of significant concern, particularly in France. But the absence of a direct European commitment there, especially following the French withdrawal from Indochina in 1954, left plenty of resources to devote to other pressing issues.

The plight of the Palestinian people, brought to global attention by Israel's conquest of the West Bank and Gaza, reentered the news cycle at the precise moment when European leftists were searching for a project complementary to their exertions of challenging the status quo at home. In a way, the situation was similar to the one facing the global Left after the dismantling of apartheid, when the energy that had been bound up with efforts to undermine the South African government from afar was suddenly free to be redirected at racist state policies elsewhere. Whatever the merits of the Palestinian cause, its appeal to European leftists did not wax because of changes in Israel's governmental and military practice, but rather because of circumstances that initially had little to do with the Israel-Palestine conflict itself.

The timing of the Six-Day War was highly unfortunate from this perspective, because it decisively reshaped public perception of Israel in Europe just when the continent's Left was primed to interpret Israel as a miniature version of the prototypical colonial power. Instead of a beleaguered outpost of hope, a testament to the survival instincts of a people that had endured the absolute worst kind of discrimination, Israel now seemed a bit of a bully. The images of triumphant Israelis, flush with martial pride, that were disseminated worldwide in the aftermath of the conflict (such as the *Life* magazine cover of an exuberant IDF solider, the photogenic Yossi Ben Hanan, cooling off in the Suez Canal with his AK-47 raised in the air) served to powerfully reinforce this perception. Israel's virility had mutated into militarism.

It was in this context that the Palestine Liberation Organization and the breakaway Popular Front for the Liberation of Palestine emerged as the darlings of the European Left. By forming savvy alliances with extremist groups such as Germany's Red Army Faction and with trade unions, usually on the basis of a shared interest in Marxism, Palestinian activists were able to establish enough of a presence on the continent that they seemed like insiders within its radical circles. Soon they had attained a status analogous to that of the Viet Cong, with the crucial difference that the Palestinians were forced to do most of their work in exile. In effect, this made Europe a home away from home, or, to be more precise, a home away from political homelessness.

Once the United States had replaced France and the United Kingdom as Israel's primary supplier of military and financial support, the attractiveness of the Palestinian cause for European leftists increased further. Scale was a factor here, just as it would later be in the wake of apartheid's dismantling. Israel seemed to offer a way of confronting American imperialism without being overwhelmed by the magnitude of the task. But in this case the process of fetishization was more obviously a reaction to the shrinking of Europe's role in world affairs. Even if the radical Left managed to achieve significant political power in countries like France, Germany, and the United Kingdom, it would represent something of a pyrrhic victory, since the United States and the Soviet Union dominated the globe. The attractiveness of Israel as a target for European leftists was therefore bound up with a broader concern—variously expressed throughout the continent—with the end of colonialism. Leftists and conservatives alike were coming to terms with the long-term consequences of the Second World War, which, in devastating much of Europe, had also delivered a deathblow to its global hegemony.

Pointing out the degree to which Israel was serving as a pawn in the global chess match between the United States and the Soviet Union was a way for leftists to displace the realization that Western Europe, despite its history, had been forced into a similarly subservient role to the U.S. Israel thus acquired two distinct, if complementary, functions in the political imagination of the European Left in the years following the Six-Day War. On the one hand, it was an outlet for nostalgia about the time when Europe dominated world affairs and the dream of a day when those glory days would return. On the other, it was a repository for anxieties about the current state of European politics, in which the continent's major nations had all been reduced to proxies of the two superpowers. Taken together, these functions burdened Israel with a great deal of psychological significance, far more than it could readily shake off.

To be sure, Israel did its best to ward off the charge of colonialism. Israeli leaders repeatedly invoked the image of the country as an isolated outpost for American-style democracy and freedom, hearkening back to the nation's early days when it could be rooted for as an underdog in constant danger of being wiped from the map. But it was not enough to prevent serious damage to the nation's self-image. Zionism is predicated on the belief that Jews have a right to return to the historic land of Palestine because they were its original inhabitants and were forcibly exiled from it by a European colonial power. If not for Roman foreign policy, the argument goes, they would probably have remained in the region and turned out to resemble something on the order of Mizrahis (Jews from Islamic nations), Palestinians, or even Kurds. In light of this understanding of Jewish history, the European critique of Zionism as a colonial enterprise smacked of the worst kind of hypocrisy.

Further muddying the waters was the fact that the story of the Palestinian exiles closely resembled the foundational narrative of the state of Israel. Sent into the Diaspora by European invaders, these stateless wanderers insisted on the same right to return as early Zionists. That the Palestinian displacement occurred within living memory may have made it more painfully visible than the one that befell the Jews under Roman rule, but that does not mean that its logic was any different. And, as the stubborn refusal of Jews to forget their ancestral homeland over two millennia makes abundantly clear, distance from a traumatic historical event is no indication of the intensity with which it is collectively felt.

During the period in which the European Left's new approach to Zionism was gaining ground, Jewish concerns that the continent was reverting to its not-so-old ways mounted. To many, the charge that Israel was a colonialist nation seemed to be just one aspect of a more comprehensive metamorphosis. Both in the West and the East, relations with the Arab world were improving. At the same time, Muslim immigration to countries like France, the United Kingdom, and West Germany was increasing at a rapid pace, suggesting that interest in the legacy of Israel in the aftermath of the Holocaust might give way to other preoccupations. And then, during the early 1970s, Europe became the principal foreign site of Palestinian revolutionary violence.

Many Jews underestimated the extent to which the discrimination they once experienced on the continent, at least prior to Hitler's rise to power, could be redirected at the Muslim populations of cities like Paris, London, and Berlin. For example, although solidarity with the Palestinians became a hallmark of French radicals in the 1960s, the French government saw little resistance to its plan to concentrate the country's new immigrants from North Africa in isolated suburbs—the infamous *banlieues*, which rivaled the worst public housing that the Eastern bloc had to offer. Still, it is understandable that Jews inclined to a pessimistic worldview believed that Europe was already well on its way by the early 1970s to becoming the primary breeding ground of a virulent "Islamo-Left." For these individuals, the years following the Six-Day War provided irrefutable proof that, outside of Israel, the United States was the only place a Jew could truly be safe.

Despite heavy Jewish representation within the leadership cadres of France's Socialist and Communist parties, their presence did little to calm fears that the French Left's new pro-Palestinian stance was a harbinger of a full-fledged anti-Semitism on the continent. Ironically, however, although anti-Jewish racism existed to varying degrees across the European Left—frequently couched in the language of Marxist universalism—the prejudice ascribed to young radicals was more likely to be found among the old-guard followers of Charles de Gaulle. As I have already noted, the perception that de Gaulle himself was an anti-Semite derived, in part, from a failure to acknowledge that his decision to suspend arms sales to Israel was motivated as much by France's disastrous final decade in Algeria as by whatever personal feelings he may have had. But that does not mean that his followers were so motivated.

The spectacular terrorist actions staged by Palestinian guerrilla organizations in Europe during the early 1970s did much to reinforce Jewish perceptions that the continent had once again become a hostile place. The scale of the Palestinian attacks on Israeli interests seemed to add muscle to the criticisms of Israel being voiced by Europeans, even if they did not represent a deeper conspiracy. More significantly, the fact that Israel had only become a nation because of what had happened in Europe in the 1930s and 1940s was conveniently forgotten.

CREATING AN ALTERNATIVE DIASPORA

Given the enormity of the losses suffered by European Jewry between 1933 and 1945, the deterioration of Israeli-European relations after the Six-Day War may seem relatively insignificant. Or, at the very least, a development that one would expect to have originated in Jewish instead of European circles. After all, Jewry had more than its fair share of reasons to reject European civilization in toto given the tragedy that had just befallen it. It can be argued that the Nazi genocide was a perverse by-product of the same historical and social developments that helped define what it means to be Western. Anti-Semitism was not a foreign import, but European through and through. And it wasn't a residue of premodern Europe, either. No, the racism expressed toward Jews from the nineteenth century onward, even as it mobilized earlier forms of anti-Semitism, went hand in hand with the outwardly rational forces of modernity. The problem for European Jews, particularly in Western Europe, is that they typically identified with these forces as well, going out of their way to convince themselves that anti-Semitism was the antithesis of modernity.

This conviction added to the difficulty of disidentifying with Europe, even after the Holocaust had demonstrated once and for all that Jews could never hope to be fully assimilated in Gentile society, however modern it seemed. From Theodore Herzl's *Der Judenstaat (The Jewish State)* onward, Zionist ideology has always regarded Jewish national identity as being culturally European. What "European" means in this context, however, is complicated. Summing up Herzl's position in the *Socialist Register*

in 1970, the Belgian Jewish Marxist thinker Marcel Liebman argues that Herzl envisioned his Israel-to-come
as a European outpost, both for practical purposes—
protection from its neighbors—and for ideological reasons. Israel would derive its legitimacy from the value it
held for Western powers in the Middle East. In the same
article, Liebman explains how this logic played itself out
in Israel's participation in the Anglo-French attempt to
seize the Suez Canal from Egypt in 1956, as well as its
support for France's attempt to retain Algeria later that
same decade. Though by no means the only goal Herzl
had for Israel's relationship with Europe—to his credit,
the Viennese journalist possessed grander ideals—this
distressing vision of the nation as an outpost in the Ori-
ent provides essential background for understanding
what happened after the Six-Day War, not to mention
the kinds of justifications Israeli neoconservatives offer
for Western support of the country's actions today. But
whatever the specific reasons that France and the United
Kingdom gave for suspending arms sales to Israel in 1967,
the aftermath of the decolonization process would eventually have led to a break anyway. Israel simply did not
hold the same value that it had when they still retained
significant portions of their respective empires.

Although it took a long time for some Israelis to come
to grips with this change, the shift initiated by Europe
after the Six-Day War was eventually reciprocated. It
is crucial to note, however, that this realignment never
took the form of an explicit rejection of European civilization or values. Despite the political changes taking
place, Israel continued to conduct an extremely high level
of nonmilitary business with Europe, and vice versa. But

the constant adversity facing Israel necessitated a close partnership with an international power. Between Palestinian guerrilla raids from Jordan; the War of Attrition, in which the IDF had daily exchanges with Egypt across the Suez Canal beginning in 1967; and, after the PLO was driven from Jordan in 1970, the initial use of Lebanon as a staging ground for attacks; along with the ever-present threat of a region-wide conflagration—Israel needed a steady supply of weapons and money.

This is when the country's special relationship with the United States really took off. Not surprisingly, American leaders tended to regard Israel's ongoing conflicts with its neighbors in terms of its own struggle with the USSR. After all, Moscow was the main backer of Syria, Egypt, and, later, the PLO. If the United States became increasingly generous to Israel as the Cold War wore on, it was not for altruistic impulses, although they were present, so much as preserving its own interests. Critics of American aid to Israel—by 2003, a number of surveys pegged expenditures at three billion dollars per year—tend to overlook this crucial fact. If the United States is being exploited in the special relationship, it is an exploitation that American leaders have actively encouraged in order to promote a broader agenda in the Middle East and beyond.

On the Israeli end, gratitude at the United States' generosity, however self-interested, was initially coupled with frustration at the perceived crassness and immaturity of its culture. Half of Israel's population was of European descent, so this mild bias made sense. Over time, though, the pros of identifying with America came to outweigh the cons. The simple fact that the United

States was fundamentally different from the traditional European powers that had broken with Israel after the Six-Day War made it an attractive alternative. By entering the orbit of the United States, Israel was given the opportunity to finally separate from the historical Diaspora.

Of course, the United States was also part of the Diaspora. As many Jews who have made *aliyah* (immigrated) to Israel will attest, almost anywhere that is not Israel is the Diaspora, including the United States. But the American Diaspora was sufficiently different from its European counterpart, despite their shared roots, to be free of the existential burden associated with that word. Most of the Jews in the United States were there because either they or their ancestors had wanted to go there. Though American history was by no means free of anti-Semitism, there were no inquisitions, death camps, pogroms, or histories of state-sponsored anti-Jewish activities. And despite a nominally Protestant demeanor, the U.S. differed from Europe in its diverse, immigration-fueled population. To the historically persecuted outsider looking in, the United States seemed thoroughly multiethnic, interfaith, and politically democratic. Although Western Europe had also demonstrated commitment to one or more of these ideals in the modern era, it was only in the wake of the Holocaust that its leading states were making a concerted effort to realize all of them together, across national boundaries.

Factor in the entrepreneurial do-it-yourself ethos that had helped distribute an unprecedented percentage of wealth to the American middle class, and you can understand why Israelis could eventually be wooed by the idea of the United States. Struggling for state-owned enterprises and collective farms had primed many of them for a more individualistic, but also tolerant, way of life. Politically socialist, with an enormous public sector equivalent to that which existed in Western European welfare states, Israel was not likely to resemble the United States anytime soon. But the political decision to embrace American sponsorship gave Israelis the opportunity to dream about a better future for themselves as individuals, even as they reaped the benefits of their tightly coordinated collective action in the present.

As simple as it would be to reduce Israel's turn toward the United States in the late 1960s as a product of the Jewish experience of Europe—a history of persecution and dependence—such an analysis would ultimately land off the mark. Although there is obviously truth to such an explanation—the sort, incidentally, that Jewish neoconservatives typically proffer—it tries too hard to make Israel match an idealized version of the United States, as I suggested earlier in the book. From this perspective, Israel is represented as the Middle East's sole democracy, committed to promoting the values of freedom and modernity, a beacon for the rest of the Middle East just as the United States once was for Europe. And the values Israel shares with the United States give the two countries common cause in protecting the rest of the world from the rising threat of "Islamo-Fascism." The story is a familiar one, because it has been drummed into us over and over since 9/11.

NEITHER EUROPE NOR AMERICA
Before the War on Terror, rhetoric about "Israeli" values was far less commonplace, although the arguments made

by the Bush administration's ideological allies were certainly not new. What changed was the willingness of
Israel's leadership to toe the party line in selling the idea
of a Pax Americana. Bush's version of the if-you-aren't-my-
friend-you're-my-enemy approach led many people to suspend judgment, including British Prime Minister Tony
Blair. But the Israeli government, given the length and
depth of its special relationship with the United States,
seemed to feel that it had been called upon to be especially supportive of its ally. It may have seemed useful for
Israel to depict itself as a European outpost in the Middle East, embracing the Western values of the time—in
this instance, those promulgated by Bush's stable of
conservative ideologues—and reproducing them locally,
just as Israel had with the foreign military equipment it
purchased and often improved. But this was more than a
shallow exercise in mimicry. It was also an ideal way to
repurpose a formulation that Israeli conservatives had
been working toward ever since the Six-Day War and
the conquest of the West Bank and Gaza: namely, that
their homeland is a modern, democratic country, where
both freedom of conscience and individual initiative are
promoted as state policy.

Even though it is officially Jewish—both "Jewish
and democratic," as the slogan goes—Israel is in practice a multiethnic and interfaith society. Within a population of over seven million people exist a multiplicity
of Jewish ethnicities, a million and a half Arabs, and almost half a million Christians. Its Basic Laws—Israel's
equivalent of a constitution—reflect this diversity in its
core legislation. Both the Supreme Court and its elected
legislators in the Knesset are entrusted to enforce equal-

ity, racial tolerance, and respect for civil rights in Israeli public life. In other words, Israel is a typically Western nation in most respects . . . but not when it comes to seeing all religious and ethnic backgrounds as functionally equal. Then again, most European nations fall short of true equality in this regard as well. The important point here is that representatives of the Israeli state *believe* that they have a mandate to let ethnic distinctions unfairly influence how the government administrates Israeli civil society.

For example, the Knesset frequently enacts legislation that contradicts the commitment to equality promised by the Basic Laws. (To wit, as the final draft of this book was being finished, a parliamentary committee banned Arab parties from participating in the February 2009 national election, only to have the decision overturned by Israel's Supreme Court.) Many critics would in fact argue that Israel's Basic Laws are not as egalitarian as Israeli liberals like to believe. Nevertheless, the Israel that exists within the country's pre-1967 boundaries can roughly be characterized as liberal-democratic.

Over 2.5 million Palestinians are estimated to live in the West Bank and Israeli-administered East Jerusalem alone. Though regarded as citizens of a future Palestinian state, for over forty years Palestinian residents of this territory have lived as a functionally stateless people, whose civil and political rights have been granted to them exclusively on the basis of Israeli security considerations. The Israeli military gradually developed its own civil administration in the territories, complete with the trappings of a shadow state apparatus, but the services provided to the Palestinian population by the civil authorities were always extremely limited; this has been exacerbated over the past two decades, first as a result of Israeli military withdrawals from Areas A and B (zones within the Occupied Territories designated by the Oslo Accords as being under full control of the Palestinian Authority, and under the security auspices of the IDF, respectively) during the 1990s, and then because of the al-Aksa Intifada, which took place between September 2000 and the spring of 2005.

While the discrepancies between Israeli and Palestinian civil rights under Israeli rule were always a primary concern of European critics of the occupation, attention shifted over the course of the al-Aksa Intifada to the sadism of Israeli settlers (the beatings of Palestinian civilians, the uprooting of their orchards) and the methods applied by Israeli security forces (administrative detentions, geographical bisections and closures, and, most dramatically, checkpoints). Extensive documentation of the effects of the separation wall, whose construction began in 2004, on the lives of Palestinian civilians helped to confirm the grim picture of Israeli hypocrisy that leftists had been drawing for some time. Just as the United States had become increasingly isolated under George W. Bush, so had Israel during his tenure.

They Might Have a Point

Interviewed by the Jerusalem Center for Public Affairs about his years serving as Israel's ambassador to Sweden, an incensed Zvi Mazel did not hesitate to characterize the historically progressive Nordic country's political class and media as being thoroughly anti-Semitic. While stationed in Stockholm between 2002 and 2004, Mazel

issued the familiar refrains that many Israeli and Jewish
conservatives have applied to European countries since
1967: The public there maintains an unhealthy obsession
with the Arab-Israeli conflict. The left-wing parties—in
Sweden's case, the Greens and the Social Democrats—
are hostile to Israel. The country's leading journalists
continue to praise Arab dictators such as Saddam Hussein. The government plays host to Muslim immigrant
extremists. And the leading "intellectual" periodicals
consistently characterize Israel as an oppressive colonialist state. Even though Mazel has a reputation for
emotional outbursts—in 2004, the ambassador made international headlines for vandalizing Israeli artist Dror
Feiler's portrayal of a dead Palestinian suicide bomber
in a pool of blood at a Stockholm museum—I still do not
want to belittle his frustrations.

As both an Israeli and an American, I can attest to
how lonely it can feel to be in Europe during a time of
conflict in the Middle East. Sitting in a cab in Madrid
during the opening days of the first Gulf War in January
1991, for example, I was subject to the single harshest political lecture I've ever received, upon telling the driver
I was Israeli (carelessly thinking that because Scud missiles were also falling on Tel Aviv, it would be better than
saying I was American). "You scum are all the same,"
he yelled in Spanish, "imperialist dogs masquerading as
Middle Easterners. You should all go back to New York
where you belong!" And that was just the opening salvo.
"Tell them you're from Toronto next time," my father,
who was then living in Madrid, said over dinner later
that evening. "It's just not worth the trouble."

Despite the fact that Israel has much to boast about

in asserting that it is a Western-style democracy, it is clear that its occupation of the territories must end before anyone will really listen and stop predicating their understanding of us on the basis of ideology. Ironically, that is precisely what Charles de Gaulle suggested in his letter to David Ben Gurion in the aftermath of the Six-Day War. Even though the French and British decisions to limit arms sales to Israel in the wake of the conflict may not have been undertaken for the best of reasons, it now seems increasingly clear that diplomatic efforts to patch up relations with those two European powers would have helped prevent a lot of the heartache that followed.

Paradoxically, an Israel less beholden to the United States, diplomatically constrained by its allies' fears of Arab opinion, might not have been as likely to go to war in Lebanon in 2006—though the EU did not, in the end, stand in Israel's way. Even if Europe really is overrun with the "Arab-loving liberals" that Israelis like Zvi Mazel rail against, that does not mean that Israel should have given up trying to work with its past ideological dictates either. By turning away from Europe so abruptly, Israel ended up engaging in its most self-destructive tendencies. As the United States has found out in Iraq and Afghanistan, long-term occupation of territory that belongs to others is the sort of operation that can make everyone involved a loser.

Chapter Seven

MOVING PICTURES

Normally, I don't pay close attention to previews when I go to the movies, but this one had me fixed on the screen from the second it started. *He is the greatest Israeli soldier the world has ever known*, an authoritative voiceover intoned, as a man in civilian clothes walked amid soldiers in classic IDF attire. The next shot showed a close-up of the same man popping a clip into an Uzi. The voice continued, with pauses for dramatic effect, as gunfire, explosions, and improbable stunts paraded across the screen. *His training is lethal. And his skills are legendary.* To many, it probably seemed like the latest example of a burgeoning subgenre, the anti-terrorism action flick. But I noticed something amiss. This supposedly matchless Jewish warrior was wearing a Mariah Carey T-shirt.

It did not surprise me when another shot of him loading a weapon followed, only this time indicating a slackening of purpose. *But it was time for a change*, the narrator added. And then we saw our protagonist, now recognizable as American comedian Adam Sandler, speaking to his parents over dinner. "I want to leave the army. I love my country," he began, his voice now accompanied by a beach scene and a line of lascivious bikini-clad women.

"But the fighting," he continued, as this Mediterranean fantasy gave way to shots of soldiers marching across a desert, an angry crowd fronted by a banner in Arabic, and what looked like the aftermath of a car bombing. When his image reappeared on the screen, he concluded with a question: "When does it end?"

Like Sandler's character, the audience in the theater was now confused. What sort of picture was this? Sandler is known for making crude comedies. So far, though, the preview had not been played for cheap laughs. Had he finally decided, like Woody Allen, Robin Williams, and Jim Carrey before him, that his career would be incomplete until he branched out into dramas? But then the preview changed course, laying out the scenario in which the type of humor Sandler is known for would be appropriate. This "greatest Israeli soldier" was not only going to leave the army, but his homeland as well. He was coming to New York City to cut hair.

Reassured, the audience began to laugh. But I could hear hesitation in the way many of them were responding. After all, we have only just now reached the point, decades after the Vietnam War ended, when a mainstream Hollywood studio felt the time was right for spoofs of pictures like *Apocalypse Now*, *Platoon*, and *Full Metal Jacket*. And there certainly aren't any comedies about 9/11 in the industry pipeline. To make a film about a conflict that is still ongoing, not to mention one that has been heavily covered in the American media, was a daring move. Perhaps, as the ambient unease in the crowd suggested, it was more than the moviegoing public was ready for.

The preview for *You Don't Mess with the Zohan* culminates in a curious scene from the film that, although humorous in nature, conveys a serious point. A well-dressed businessman, the sort we associate with Wall Street—and the sort that perished in droves in the destruction of the World Trade Center—angrily confronts Adam Sandler's character for a transgression we do not witness. "Stay out of my business, Mustafa," he declares. Sandler looks bemused as he replies, "This is not my name." He then responds to the insult by punishing his interlocutor with martial arts techniques, filmed to look as silly as possible. But the fact that the businessman is either unwilling or unable to distinguish Israelis from Arabs gives the humor an edge. While dishing out punches, Sandler captures the existential condition of the average American who, in the wake of 9/11, suddenly realized that the world could no longer be kept at a distance. In this context, the distinction between friend and foe mattered less than the sense that our personal space had been irrevocably violated.

When I did end up seeing the film upon its theatrical release, other scenes that thematize transgression reinforced the impression that distance had crumpled into proximity. The film, which tells the tale of a top Mossad agent who fakes his own death in order to realize his dream of becoming a hairdresser in the United States and, he hopes, leave the burdens of his past behind, is consistently silly, but with an edge that sets it apart from other Sandler vehicles. His character, Zohan, conforms to the international stereotype of Israelis as people who, whatever their good qualities, suffer from severe boundary problems. Single-minded in pursuing his professional goals, whether they involve knocking off a Palestinian terrorist or taking his Palestinian boss at the hair salon out on a date, he strides purposefully into territory where others fear to tread. It is no coincidence, then, that the film does the same thing. By refusing to heed concerns about what audiences are ready for, *You Don't Mess with the Zohan* positions itself as the hardheaded Israeli to Hollywood's more timid American products.

It is highly significant, therefore, that the film is an American production. In encouraging the audience to identify with an Israeli over Americans like the businessman who can only see Mustafas, it crosses a line that few post–9/11 Hollywood pictures have dared to approach. Although the number of films openly critical of the United States government increased with each year that George W. Bush was in office, they almost always featured a tried-and-true formula in which an American protagonist comes to recognize that the nation's authority figures are betraying the public's trust. In *You Don't Mess with the Zohan*, on the other hand, it is not the American government but the average American moviegoer who is put on the spot. The willful ignorance we cultivated prior to 9/11 is presented as a major problem; the humor in the film insists that we need to work harder to see the world through eyes that are both less naïve and more innocent.

More broadly, *You Don't Mess with the Zohan* is a reminder—all the more powerful for having come from an unexpected corner—that newspapers and television channels like CNN need not be the only source of information about what matters to us. Particularly when the news is so constrained by ritual that it often seems the antithesis of serious reporting, other forms of cultural production may prove to be more effective at reshaping our worldviews. Novels and films are sometimes the only way to attain a fresh perspective.

That *Zohan* was later the subject of a hotly discussed attack in the journal *Azure* by the future ambassador to the U.S., Michael B. Oren, only served to underline the film's political prescience. Especially considering the fact that Oren's article, "Zohan and the Quest for Jewish Utopia," contends that Sandler's film, beloved, as Oren correctly notes, by Israelis across the political spectrum, "more than any other work of popular entertainment, and certainly one produced by Jews . . . repudiates the Zionist idea."

ZIONIST AGITPROP

In the winter of 2005, posters extolling Israel's liberal political credentials began appearing on trains, buses, and at public transit stops in San Francisco. Touting everything from Israel's encouragement of the rights of Arab women to vote in the country's elections to its steadfast commitment to freedom of the press, the campaign struck me as a response to developments like the Rainbow Grocery discussion in which I had participated at the height of the al-Aksa Intifada.

Produced by the firm BlueStarPR, the advertisements were remarkably savvy. One featured an image of "indigenous" Arab Jews at Jerusalem's Western Wall in 1925, belying the notion that modern-day Israel was strictly a post–World War II invention. Another was a portrait of an identifiably "out" IDF soldier suggestively pimping his vintage Uzi. The extent that these ads targeted particular San Francisco demographics was striking. This was not a national campaign along the lines of those I discussed in Chapter Three, such as the semi-pornographic *Maxim* feature on female Israeli soldiers. The care and expense taken to win over local opinion was impressive indeed. But that did not make me any less suspicious of the advertisements' purpose. Although I admit to being stirred by these portraits, I felt that they were primarily a defensive gesture. Instead of truly promoting the liberal aspects of Israel, they were merely serving to distract liberals in California.

Over the course of the al-Aksa Intifada, media imagery of soldiers abusing Palestinians at checkpoints and children getting killed by IDF fire had helped to promulgate an international perception of Israel as a ruthless colonial enterprise run by racist religious fanatics wearing military uniforms. Seeking to raise consciousness of the plight of the Palestinians, the frequently excessive rhetoric of the antioccupation movement had threatened to turn this representation of Israel into a new norm, a negative stereotype instead of the complex picture that I had devoted my own work to disseminating. Now, with the BlueStar campaign, here was an attempt to counter that oversimplification, but one that was just as propagandistic.

Paradise Now

After writing a column about BlueStar's campaign for *Tikkun* magazine, I received a message from the firm a couple of months later thanking me for the exposure I had given their work. And then I forgot about them. But when I started to do research for this chapter, I unexpectedly encountered the group in a different context. While collecting reports on the American response to the film *Paradise*

Now, I learned of a poster commissioned by BlueStar in which a photo of Hany Abu-Assad, the film's Palestinian-Israeli director, was featured alongside a quotation from him. And not just any quotation, either, but one excerpted from an interview with Abu-Assad that I had published in the online edition of *Tikkun*.

Conducted by journalist Tirzah Agassi, a former columnist for the *Jerusalem Post* and the granddaughter of the best-known Jewish proponent of a binational Palestinian-Israeli state, the late theologian and philosopher Martin Buber, the interview was interesting in its own right. I could see why BlueStar had paid it such close attention. Soon, though, my initial delight at seeing the fruits of my labor so ably repurposed turned to consternation. As I examined the image more closely, I noticed that the quotation seemed different from the one I remembered. Maybe I was just being paranoid, but the sort of liberties people sometimes take in quoting statements on controversial topics can be especially damaging in the atmosphere of constant tension that surrounds discussion of the Israel-Palestine conflict. I had to check.

The BlueStar poster had Abu-Assad making a programmatic statement about the importance of Jewish culture: "The Jews have always been the conscience of humanity, always, wherever they go . . . Ethics. Morality. They invented it! I think Hitler wanted to kill the conscience of the Jews, the conscience of humanity. But this conscience is still alive . . . Thank God!" In the original interview, however, the quote did indeed read differently: "The Jews have been the conscience of humanity, always, wherever you go. Not all Jews, but part of them. Ethics, morality. You invented it! I think Hitler wanted to kill the conscience of the Jews, the conscience of humanity. But this conscience is still alive . . . Maybe a bit weak . . . but still alive. Thank God!"

The similarity between these quotes is deceptive. On the surface, the BlueStar version of Abu-Assad's statement appears to be a simple abridgement of the director's words. No doubt, that is what the firm would have labeled it if pressed for an explanation. Unfortunately, though, in paring this statement down, BlueStar had removed the crucial qualifications that Abu-Assad took pains to make in the interview. Not all Jews are committed to being morally self-conscious, according to the director, and some demonstrate a "weak" conscience. In BlueStar's version, by contrast, there is no ambiguity at all. Jews are represented as having been uniformly good throughout history.

Something is very wrong with this picture. In order to do a service to the Israeli cause, a Zionist public relations firm doctors a quote taken from an interview with an Israeli-born Palestinian filmmaker. Discussing his latest feature, the director tells the journalist that he does not believe that "all Jews are bad," but, in fact, that they have frequently "served as humanity's conscience." Not all of them, but a good many. His implicit point, obviously, is that Israel's treatment of the Palestinians is out of character with the way that Jews have historically treated Gentiles. Considering how much the Palestinians have suffered since Israel's creation in 1948, it is hard to imagine a more reasoned, open-minded statement.

None of Abu-Assad's points seem particularly controversial unless, of course, your worldview has no room for reasonable Palestinians. If Abu-Assad is relegated by definition to the category of "enemy," however, his doctored words read not like a thoughtful meditation on how Israel has broken with the religious tradition on which it was founded, but an outright surrender to superior forces. Of course, Abu-Assad spoke these words in conversation with an Israeli journalist, on assignment for a Jewish American magazine. But that sort of contextual information, crucial to understanding Abu-Assad's arguments, is precisely what might undermine the message of the poster.

For BlueStar's purposes, it was necessary to mobilize the stereotype of an artist spouting Islamic rhetoric about crusaders, or equating Zionism with racism. When "critics" of Israel such as Abu-Assad make pronouncements that do not conform to the preconception of Palestinians as outspoken extremists, the temptation is to regard their words as a military defeat. So, even though the director's statement could not be reconfigured to make him sound like a typically hyperbolic militant, it could be subtly but decisively refashioned to make it seem as if he had broken ranks with his community. There is something deeply troubling in such a move, because it shows no respect for the subtle qualifications that mean so much in reasoned political discourse.

Without a doubt, BlueStar's charged endeavor was ingenious, a testament to how the "culture jamming" once confined to progressive publications like *Adbusters* has gradually been adapted for other types of ideological work. The point is that nothing is inviolable. In time-honored fashion, conservatives conspicuously copied the imaginative schemes of their liberal rivals, and put them to equally pointed and propitious use. Of even greater significance, though, is that such sophisticated attempts to combat "anti-Israel" bias indicate just how seriously the nation's supporters in the Diaspora have come to regard threats to its reputation from the Left. Has the Jewish state become such a divisive force that measures like these are now considered appropriate?

To many critics of the Jewish Right, the polarization of public opinion about Israel is as much the result of conservatives' reflexive denunciation of any and all opponents of the nation's policies as it is a direct reflection of what actually happens there. What these handful of BlueStar initiatives indicate, however, is that reflexive denunciation has been supplemented or perhaps even supplanted by an approach that, instead of excoriating progressives for being anti-Semites, seeks to weaken the figures they turn to in order to bolster their arguments. As someone instinctively distrusted on ethnic grounds, even though he is an Israeli citizen, the only use Abu-Assad can have in BlueStar's campaign is one that reduces his legitimacy as a critic of Israel. BlueStar turned him into a poster boy in order to diminish his usefulness for Israel's critics on the Left.

As pernicious as this move was, it at least testified to the impact that a film like *Paradise Now* can have on foreign audiences. Although bound to reach many millions fewer than a Hollywood production like *You Don't Mess with the Zohan*, Abu-Assad's picture resonated far beyond the circles of those who obsessively seek out news about the Middle East. The first Israeli film to win a Golden Globe Award since 1972, *Paradise Now* tells the story of two Palestinian men in Nablus, friends since childhood, who volunteer to be suicide bombers but find their resolve tested by the brutal consequences of that fateful decision. The direction is tense and compelling—regardless of one's stance on the conflict it thematizes. In the United States, the picture's effect was especially pronounced, since most Americans have historically exhibited little awareness of the differences between countries in the region, much less the individuals caught up in specific crises within them.

In providing a context for understanding what transpired prior to 9/11, *Paradise Now* provoked thoughtful responses to the plight of those desperate souls who turn to terrorism because they can think of no way of improving their everyday lives short of ending them. This is why it posed such a threat to Israel's strongest supporters in the Diaspora. In showing the other side, it opens viewers' eyes to the limitations of the mainstream news media in a way that no scholarly article or polemic ever can. Together with other recent films concerning the Israel-Palestine conflict, it points the way toward redefining "public relations" in a new light.

WALK ON WATER AND MUNICH

In addition to *Paradise Now*, 2005 witnessed the American release of two other films that presented the post–Six-Day War policies and practices of the Israeli government in a most unfavorable light. Israeli director Eytan Fox's second feature film, *Walk on Water*, is a homoerotic drama about a burned-out Mossad agent charged with the task of liquidating a wheelchair-bound Nazi war criminal. The film is a multilayered indictment of the profound personal price that Israel's permanent state of war continues to exact upon its increasingly damaged citizenry. Fox's film landed in American art house theaters, however briefly, to a curious combination of both bewildered and laudatory reviews. Despite its limited theatrical release, the film received enough press to ensure at least some interest when it appeared on DVD. Inadvertently, it also turned out to be the first installment in a trilogy of like-minded films about Israel that year, rounded out with *Paradise Now* and *Munich*—Steven Spielberg's picture about the Israeli retaliation for the massacre of its athletes at the 1972 Olympics.

Despite their obvious differences, it appeared as though the three directors—Fox, Abu-Assad, and Steven Spielberg—shared two basic, overarching convictions about the Israeli-Palestinian conflict: that violence as a political tool only perpetuates more violence, and that when politics is motivated by the desire for revenge, it inevitably results in self-destruction. If that sounds like a Greek tragedy getting played out in Middle Eastern drag, the suspicion is not misplaced. For decades now, the region has staged political dramas in which hubris invariably leads to someone's downfall. The Bush administration's prosecution of the Iraq War is but one recent example. Yet these three films tackle the archetype with enough skill and conviction to give even the most threadbare narrative template new life.

In *Walk on Water*, Israel's military echelon is shown to be deeply self-absorbed, lacking in any governing principle other than repetition of a tired pattern. Without a trace of political leadership, the most it can offer are the targeted assassinations of Palestinian militants and aging European war criminals. In *Paradise Now*, the Palestinian revolutionary commanders are shown to be similarly bankrupt, deceiving young men into killing themselves in exchange for a place in heaven. Using a worldly, young Palestinian aid worker to deliver his verdict to a prospective martyr, Abu-Assad's indictment of suicide bombing as a revolutionary strategy is clear and unequivocal, even if, in the end, it fails to prevent the young man from undertaking his mission. Likewise, in *Munich*, the pursuit of revenge at any price also demonstrates a failure to see into the future, as the people responsible for hunting down the terrorists end up resembling their prey.

Coming at a time of heightened fighting in Iraq, and the start of massive public debate in both the United States and the United Kingdom over the price being paid for the war, these films were like votes of no-confidence from every major national player in the region: Israelis, Americans, and Arabs. Though focused on the Israeli-Palestinian conflict, all three films had much larger audiences in mind. To understand where responses like BlueStar's treatment of Abu-Assad come from, it is crucial to recognize the cumulative effect these works had on their audiences. For the first time, words like "occupation" were being bandied about to describe the American presence in Iraq, displacing the term from its Israeli-specific context—indeed, for many on the Left, the two occupations blurred into one—and also suggesting that the plight of the Palestinians might stand in for the conditions faced by Muslims throughout the region.

By January 2006, *Paradise Now* had been nominated for an Academy Award (in the Best Foreign Language Film category) and *Munich* had garnered five nominations.

Though neither would go on to win any awards—the protests against their respective category nominations were quite intense—both had left an undeniable mark on the minds of an increasingly agitated American public. *Walk on Water*, by contrast, received comparatively little attention. Although the film was seen by many in the Diaspora, particularly on the Left, it never reached the broader audience that made *Paradise Now* into a minor independent hit. Was it because Fox's film was the only one of the three directed by an Israeli Jew? Did the story's queer content keep it out of certain theaters? Whatever the reason, the film's relative neglect was unfortunate because it delivered the most nuanced critique of the three.

Walk on Water opens with the assassination of an exiled Hamas official in front of his wife and young son on an Istanbul ferry dock. The film's troubled protagonist, Eyal, seems to kill anything he comes into contact with. Indeed, as the archetypal macho Israeli male—the sort of figure that Adam Sandler was clearly caricaturing in *You Don't Mess with the Zohan*—Eyal is the epitome of national toxicity. Returning triumphantly home from the Turkish operation, he finds that his beautiful young wife has committed suicide. She had left behind a note accusing him of having an inescapably fatal personality. At this point, director Fox's politics become quite clear.

The film goes on to chart a transformation in Eyal that might serve as an example for real-world Israelis eager to escape the cycle of death. It is in Eyal's relationship with Axel, the grandson of a Nazi he is tasked with liquidating—and a gay, politically correct, German teacher with a proclivity for cute Palestinian club kids—that the Israeli eventually starts to soften, under-going a metamorphosis that allows him to embrace the importance of such stereotypically "un-Israeli" things as private life, intimate relationships, and open dis-plays of emotion. And, in keeping with recent trends, Eyal's transformation comes to a head in Europe, the place increasing numbers of Israelis are turning to in the hopes of discovering a collective identity not bound to the United States. Finally in position to complete his mission, Eyal backs away from the task. "I can't kill any-more," he moans, laying his head on Axel's chest as the tears begin to flow.

Although the film's narrative meanders more than my summary suggests, *Walk on Water* aims directly at its ideological target. Everything that happens to soften Eyal represents an assault on the stereotype of Israeli masculinity he embodies. For director Eytan Fox, the failures of Zionism are directly connected to a rejection of sensitivity to pain, whether of oneself, one's friends, or one's enemies. In classic nationalist fashion, male sexuality in Israel has been harnessed for specific politi-cal ends, ones that inevitably put the needs of the state before those of the individual.

This is not to deny that the nation's history has dic-tated the need for certain kinds of repression in times of crisis. The problem, however, is that Israel's lead-ers long ago lost the will to distinguish between real crises and other situations not quite as extreme. Like the post–9/11 United States, which followed in its dubi-ous footsteps, Israel is a nation imprisoned in a state of permanent emergency. In asking its citizens and, more specifically, its men to defer their feelings until a later, safer date, the country has ended up hardening them to the point where only extreme circumstances, such as the suicide of Eyal's wife, have the power to break through the security perimeter that individuals maintain around their hearts. Authority figures in government demand sacrifices, reflexes instead of thoughtfulness. The result is a state of mind in which violence is not the exception, but the rule.

By situating Eyal's transformation in Germany, with Palestinian suicide bombers routinely detonating themselves against an Israeli background, *Walk on Water* asks whether a country that exacts such a toll can truly be considered the salvation of the people the Holocaust threatened to exterminate. The body can live on long after the spirit is extinguished. Could it be that Israel's body politic is in a coma? Explaining his motivations for directing the film in a press release published by his American distributor, Fox confirms the significance of his having chosen Germany as the site to ask such a dramatic question. Arguing that Israeli men are reared to be so strong as to be Holocaust-proof, Fox invokes the timeworn "Never again!" slogan. Israelis, he argues, have been turned into unfeeling, homicidal monsters not all that dissimilar from their late European tormentors. Or, to put it in more parochial terms, typified by the attributes ascribed to a good many Israeli men: inarticulate, reactionary, and lacking a sense of humor.

As predictable as this critique of Israeli masculinity may seem—certainly, it is one that has been made many times before—the fact that *Walk on Water* was produced during the height of the al-Aksa Intifada gives Fox's charges additional weight. Contending that such a troubled manliness needs a permanent state of conflict in order to sustain itself, Fox sees his film as a challenge to a self-destructive national ethos that requires the victims of Nazism to continually will themselves into playing the role of their former persecutors. What began as an injunction to prevent the horrors that befell the Jews during Hitler's reign, a refusal to submit to brutality, has morphed into a refusal to advance beyond the insistence on self-preservation at all costs, including the destruction of individual selfhood. "Never again!" thereby becomes a perverse parody of its original meaning, signaling not only a desire to prevent the past from being repeated, but also a commitment to prevent the future from arriving. What Fox seems to want to say, even to the point of risking the charge that he is deaf to the suffering of actual Palestinians, is that Israel's greatest enemy is stationed within the minds of its citizens.

In *Walk on Water*'s closing scenes, we find Eyal approaching a crib to care for a crying baby. As the camera tracks his movements, we soon realize that he is sharing a house on a kibbutz with Pia, his new partner—who happens to be Axel's sister. Axel, however, is never very far away. Sitting in front of his laptop with a cup of hot tea after pacifying the newborn child, a now domesticated Eyal composes an e-mail to Axel in which he tells his brother-in-law of a fantasy he had about the two of them defying gravity by walking together across the Sea of Galilee. Obviously, while the homoerotic feelings Eyal demonstrated toward Axel earlier in the film have not gone away, settling down with the blond-haired and blue-eyed granddaughter of a Nazi on an Israeli collective settlement may represent a dramatic step forward for the former killer. But it is Eyal's unrequited desire for Pia's brother in Berlin that represents a yearning for something even more transgressive of the code of masculinity that held him prisoner at the beginning of the picture.

Ideologically speaking, *Walk on Water* is anything but simple. Could Eyal's inability to fully come out of the closet be a sexual metaphor for a future peace between Palestinians and Israelis that is correspondingly incomplete? A two-state as opposed to a one-state solution, where Jews could finally make their peace, not only with the Europe that persecuted them, but also with the Palestinians they have persecuted in turn? Fox ends the film without pinning its allegorical content down. At the very least, though, *Walk on Water* makes it clear that the individual desires that inform sexual satisfaction cannot be separated from the collective desires that constitute the political sort. On the contrary, it suggests that true liberation must realize both simultaneously.

As conventional as *Walk on Water*'s queerness will appear to those familiar with the major tenets of postmodern theory, in which gender and nationalism are frequently said to inform each other, the introduction of this sensibility into a mainstream film centered on the Israel-Palestine conflict—one which cheerfully concedes to its audience's desire for *narrative* satisfaction—marks an important turning point. In this respect, the film bears some resemblance to *Brokeback Mountain*, which sought to take the tamer fare of gay and lesbian film festivals and make it appealing to American moviegoers who would otherwise be unlikely to countenance the story of two "real men" in love. Given the iconic status that cowboys hold in American mythology, the potential disruption to mainstream common sense was analogous to the effect Fox was aiming for with the film.

In *Walk on Water*'s case, however, thematizing sexual and political union between former enemies radicalizes this message. Imagine a *Brokeback Mountain* in which one of the two men was a Native American and you can grasp just how revolutionary the implications of Fox's film actually are. Attraction to the other contradicts the prohibitions against miscegenation that cement the ideological stance on which Israel was founded. The implication is that all the rhetoric about there being an ancient war of civilizations cannot stand up against the force of sexual attraction once it is acknowledged openly. It is this message that makes a film like *Walk on Water* profoundly subversive.

Consider the context: such interventions would not be necessary if it were not for the fact that support for the occupation, and Israel's policies toward its own domestic Arab population, remains largely predicated on a persistent misrepresentation of what fuels violence against Israelis. For example, in response to Axel asking him if suicide bombing is an act of desperation, Eyal mechanically replies, "What's to think? They're animals . . ." Hence, the raison d'être for films like *Walk on Water*. They are deliberate exercises in counterpropaganda that use popular genres—in this case the spy thriller—to circumvent the political reflexes that shape response to the news.

What BlueStarPR did in modifying Hany Abu-Assad's words was to make the same point that Eyal does before his transformation, when he is still a hardened soldier unable to see people as anything but problems. From their campaign's perspective, the Palestinian director could not be speaking truthfully because his kind is not accountable to reason. The difference, of course, is that BlueStar's response to the al-Aksa Intifada was formulated in the United States, not Israel, and the people doing the actual communicating were not Israelis but Americans attempting to demonstrate a gesture of support toward their beleaguered Jewish cousins.

About two-thirds of the way through *Munich*, Avner Kauffman, the leader of the Mossad team responsible for killing the perpetrators of the Olympic massacre, finds himself outside an Athens safe house, sharing a smoke with a member of a Black September cell to which he had accidentally been assigned. Because Avner is posing as a member of Germany's Red Army Faction, the Palestinian regards him as a fellow revolutionary, a true comrade. The irony of the situation is of course undeniable. Describing a future scenario in which the world finally wakes up to Israel's true nature, the Palestinian tells Avner, "The world will start to see how they've made us into animals, and they'll start to ask questions about the conditions in our cages."

The continuity between this scene in *Munich* and the one in *Walk on Water* is clear, though the contexts differ. In one instance, we have a Jew using the term "animal" to denigrate the Palestinian people as a whole, and in another, we have a Palestinian using it to describe his own people's condition as a result of their treatment by Israel. The fact that both Israeli and Jewish American filmmakers come at this loaded stereotype from different yet equally critical places speaks volumes about what

constitutes a slowly but surely evolving set of shared Israeli American values.

Even in the pro-Israel posters one may encounter on
the streets of San Francisco, there is more depth to the
propaganda than meets the eye. When Israel is praised
for promoting the rights of Arab women to vote, for the
ability of gays to serve openly in the Israeli military, or
for inspiring leftist Palestinian directors to praise the
Jewish commitment to morality, these examples testify
less to the reality of actually existing Israel than they do
to the dream of a nation that has yet to achieve its potential. Until "Never again!" is supplanted by a slogan
more conducive to making progress, however, it seems
unlikely that this ideal will be reached anytime soon.

WE ARE ALL ZOHAN

You Don't Mess with the Zohan was no summer blockbuster.
Although it eventually broke even at the box office, it
surely disappointed those people in the film industry
whose sole preoccupation is the bottom line. But for
Adam Sandler, the project was truly a labor of love.
First conceived prior to 9/11, then put on hold for years
in the immediate wake of the terrorist attacks, it would
have been easy to abandon for less edgy, more com-
mercially promising fare. Like the character he plays,
though, Sandler was too intent on realizing his dream
to be deterred.

But what dream was it, precisely? It's worth recalling the notorious case of Jerry Lewis's never-released
1972 film *The Day the Clown Cried*. The story of a down-on-
his-luck German clown sent to a concentration camp for
mocking Hitler, it concludes with a notorious scene in

which Lewis's character, in an effort to win his freedom, leads Jewish children into the gas chamber and then, realizing what he has done, stays inside to die with them. Described by some of the few people who have seen it as one of the best examples of poor taste in the history of cinema, the film is regularly held up as an example of how comedians can go astray when they tackle serious material.

Sandler certainly knows of the film's existence. Yet rather than regarding it as a cautionary tale, he instead seems to have been inspired to prove that it is not only possible to make comedy out of material of that order, but desirable to do so. *You Don't Mess with the Zohan* is proud of its poor taste. Indeed, the film goes out of its way to make audiences think about the relationship between taste and politics.

Zohan's sense of belonging comes from a devotion to timeless pleasures of the body—sex, food, and fashion— rather than the demands of history. In the end, his affection for hummus, as opposed to more traditional markers of Jewish identity, is an indication that he refuses to be hemmed in by the political reflexes developed in the wake of the Holocaust. As an Israeli who audiences are encouraged to identify with, he also serves as an inspiration for people in the United States to move beyond their unhealthy fixation on the trauma of 9/11.

In a superlative *New York Times* review, A.O. Scott observes that the film seems dedicated to violating as many taboos as possible. "The movie is principally interested in establishing its main character as a new archetype in the annals of Jewish humor. He's a warrior and also, to an extent undreamed of in the combined works of

Philip Roth, Woody Allen, and Howard Stern, a sexual hedonist, so utterly free of neurosis or inhibition that it's hard to imagine him and Sigmund Freud occupying the same planet, much less the same cultural-religious tradition."

In other words, instead of "Never again!" Sandler's character lives the injunction to "Do it again." And it is for this reason that, unlike the protagonist of *The Day the Clown Cried*, he is able to keep us laughing past the gas chambers where the Final Solution awaits and lead us forward into a salon where the only canisters are filled with mousse.

WHOSE WAR IS IT ANYWAY?

As 2008 came to a close, Israeli director Ari Folman's animated film *Waltz with Bashir* was attracting rave reviews across the United States. Even at the height of the awards season leading up to the Oscars, when most self-consciously "important" films are released—a season significantly shortened by the 2008 presidential election—*Waltz with Bashir*, which chronicles the painful memories of IDF soldiers who served in the first Lebanon war, made a powerful impression and won a Golden Globe Award for Best Foreign Language Film. It didn't hurt that the timing of Israel's incursion into Gaza served as a perverse publicity campaign, almost exactly coinciding with the film's U.S. release.

Even so, the fact that *Waltz* is actually about its director, Ari Folman, and his struggle to determine his own complicity in a war crime—in this case the murder of 800 Palestinian civilians in Beirut's Sabra and Shatila camps in 1982—made the movie far more meaningful for its viewers than its coincidence with renewed Israeli-Palestinian violence. *Waltz with Bashir* focuses, like *Walk on Water*, on the brittleness of soldiers' stoic façades, and this was surely a boon for Diaspora audiences as well. The basic lesson of the film—that the experience of war gives you no peace, even in so-called "peacetime"—perfectly fit the dark mood of George W. Bush–era America.

The increased psychological proximity of Israel and the United States has had profound cultural effects along with the political ones. To an unprecedented extent, Americans are prepared to identify with protagonists from the Middle East and, more specifically, Israel. This, ultimately, is why *You Don't Mess with the Zohan* finally and improbably made it to the screen as a major Hollywood release. And this is also why, as I have suggested, it makes sense for us to pay as close attention to the light entertainment it offers as we do to the serious fare of the other films I've mentioned. On the surface, they may seem to have little in common with Sandler's picture. But they share an underlying message: the violence of the past intrudes on the present, no matter how far we go to evade it.

CHAPTER EIGHT

ISRAEL VS. UTOPIA

ANNIVERSARY PARTY FOR ONE

On May 8, 2008, Israel celebrated the sixtieth anniversary of its founding. Unlike the country's fiftieth birthday, commemorated in the lingering afterglow of the Oslo Accords, this was a somber occasion. Instead of looking back on the nation's remarkable achievements, many commentators preferred to look ahead, musing on its future. Some even wondered aloud whether Israel *has* a future, exposing themselves to the ritual denunciations of its staunch supporters in the Diaspora.

Everything I have done as a writer and editor on the subject of Israel, culminating in this book, has been devoted to the notion that what the world needs now is not just love—though love never hurts—but love that can pry itself free of clichés. Sometimes, as I suggested in discussing recent films about Israel in the previous chapter, eluding one cliché requires embracing another. But that doesn't mean that the battle against clichés is doomed to failure. I still believe fiercely enough in the project of Enlightenment to think that it is better to know what you're doing, even if you can't stop doing it. And I simply couldn't see a way to comment on the celebration without resorting to the very clichés I most wanted to avoid.

So I kept putting off thoughts about the anniversary, halfheartedly promising those who had asked that I would at least manage to honor the day somehow. In the end, though, all I could do was write about why I couldn't write. The best way I could think of celebrating Israel was to go out for Middle Eastern food in my neighborhood and reflect on how much better the political landscape in that region would look if its inhabitants could simply recognize the truth in Brillat-Savarin's famous observation—that we are what we eat.

COMFORT FOOD

Over the course of writing this book, I have sustained both body and mind by seeking out the cuisine of my distant homeland. The task has grown progressively easier too, as if the Middle East were trying to make things simpler by coming to my doorstep. During my final two years in San Francisco, every few months I would find a new Arab restaurant where I could sate my appetite for kibbe, falafel, and, yes, hummus. There's the Truly Mediterranean falafel parlor on 16th and Valencia, the wonderful Old Jerusalem on Mission and 26th, and a host of other spots throughout the city. Or, if I were in the mood for a drive, I would head down to San Bruno's Mideast Market on El Camino Real. Carrying everything from Ahmad Ceylon tea and fresh pita to Marcel Khalife CDs and Elite Turkish coffee, the store would both soothe and strengthen my homesickness. The guy who runs the place is from Bethlehem. I like him. And I like even more the fact that in the San Francisco Bay Area, I didn't have to make it through a security barrier or risk serious injury to make a connection with him.

He is homesick too. So is everyone else I would talk to at these eateries and shops. But it's an especially poignant homesickness, because most of the time the home that they long for has either been destroyed or was never fully imagined within their lifetimes. It is a home, in other words, that functions the way the word "Israel" has functioned for so many people over the years, whether in Lithuania or Ethiopia, Mississippi or Jamaica. A home, in short, that inspires longing less for what was than for what one day might be.

For the Arabs I talked to, of course, the name they give to this nowhere is assuredly not Israel. On the contrary, Israel is the name of the apparatus that prevents this home from finally being realized. Whether Israel is the name to which we attribute our aspirations or the name of what denies them, it is bound up with the very idea of homesickness in ways that many of my American friends simply cannot fathom.

Last year I began bringing a camera along on these trips. I would document the signs above markets and restaurants, the multilingual advertisements that testify to the city's increasingly international character, and, most significantly, those moments when divergent realities come together in a riot of accidental significance. Increasingly, local knowledge is the opposite of provincial. It is global too.

Lost in the Supermarket?

That's the argument I had tried to make at the Rainbow Grocery, when I spoke at the meeting to discuss whether a boycott of Israeli goods should be implemented as a storewide policy. Even then, several years before the latest wave of immigration from the Middle East had transformed my part of San Francisco into a pretty convincing stand-in for an established Arab neighborhood in Brooklyn or Los Angeles, it was obvious to me that the well-meaning progressives sounding off on the Israel-Palestine conflict could arrive at nuanced positions if they spent more time seeking knowledge down on Mission Street instead of in periodicals.

While many Jews find themselves enraged by the very idea that the staff of an independent grocery store would vote on a boycott—"Who do they think they are, the government?" a friend asked me afterward—they would profit by exploring what inspires such actions. The fetishization of Israel, which has increased in both frequency and intensity since 9/11, testifies principally to the frustration Americans experience at feeling excluded from decision-making at home.

Political awareness is almost always farsighted, and the Americans who invest their energy in worrying about the Israel-Palestine conflict are no exception. It is no accident that leftists in the United States started paying closer attention to the topic just as the American government, preoccupied with its own agenda, stopped doing so. The Bush administration's hands-off approach to the conflict, in sharp contrast to that of the administrations that preceded it, cried out for initiatives to be undertaken in civil society.

It wasn't simply the Bush administration's disregard for the Israel-Palestine conflict that elevated it to a central cause of the post–9/11 American Left, of course, but it sure helped. Indeed, for all the anger that the administration's neglect of the region inspired, it may have in the end cleared a pathway to intervention. Progressives were already struggling with a profoundly limited sense of agency. In the absence of government involvement, however, they found it easier to imagine their actions having a direct effect on the situation in Israel and Palestine.

As the decade wore on, American political opinions about the conflict appeared to be significantly less hampered by the poorly informed provincialism that both Israelis and Europeans have long ascribed to the United States. Whether or not one agrees with the positions that Americans started adopting as a consequence of their interest in the topic is not important. What matters is that we take that investment seriously, understanding that it is the result of the Middle East's increasing prominence in the psychological life of the United States, and that we then strive to perceive how this familiarity intersects with the nation's political traditions.

From the perspective of American progressives, steeped in the history of the civil rights movement, Israeli multiculturalism is bound to be compromised by violations of the civil rights of Palestinians residing in the Occupied Territories. Most Americans find it extremely difficult to distinguish between discriminatory practices in the territories and the more subtle ones that prevail within Israel proper. For example, the refusal of rented properties to Israeli Arabs in Tel Aviv and forced evictions of Palestinians from central Hebron are often regarded as different expressions of the same basic logic. No matter how much I try to explain the major differences between the two situations, I repeatedly find myself stymied by this impulse to generalize.

The United States is, after all, a country founded on abstractions. And Americans, despite their historical aversion to anything that lacks practical value, still tend to approach politics in abstract terms. Tip O'Neill's famous insistence that "All politics is local" may have represented a great strategy for winning campaigns, but it did not speak to the way Americans of all ideological persuasions conceptualize their convictions. Even the most naked forms of self-interest are likely to be imagined in grand terms like "freedom" and "equality."

This is why it seemed natural for the Rainbow Grocery's staff to be discussing a boycott of Israeli goods without the slightest concern that such an action might appear hypocritical. To be sure, they were looking at the Israel-Palestine conflict through a distorting glass, the product of their political education in a country where race is the first topic of concern. And they were doing so without wringing their hands about the racial politics of San Francisco, including the fact that the projects on the other side of the hill hold one of the city's largest concentrations of poor African Americans. There's something depressing about such reverse myopia. But if we confront it from the right angle, we can find a redeeming quality to it as well.

In the American Left, the slogan "Think globally, act locally" has been repeated for so long that it has lost its power to illuminate a course of action. More often than not, progressives resemble the philosophers of Karl Marx's famous eleventh thesis on Feuerbach, thinking so hard that their capacity to undertake action atrophies into a failure of will. Just as the hardened Israeli soldiers of films like *Walk on Water* and *You Don't Mess with the Zohan* have spent so much time honing their reflexes that they struggle to consider the contexts in which they had to rely on them, American progressives have spent so much time honing their powers of reflection that every move they contemplate must be routed through a hall of mirrors before it is commenced. Too often, they spend so much time peering into this hall of mirrors that the time to act expires.

What events like the Rainbow Grocery discussion demonstrate is that after years of paralysis, focusing on the conflict between Israel and Palestine was a way for progressives to make the blood start flowing back into their political reflexes. If they could take the next step of realizing that the distance that enables them to feel productive is already an outdated illusion (remembering, for example, the racial inequity within their own cities), they might make headway toward truly meaningful political action.

NOT EVERY IDENTITY CRISIS IS A CRISIS

As I was completing the final touches to this book, the Left's romance with President Barack Obama appeared to be heading down a rocky path from one crisis to the next. Although progressives had joined in the collective sigh of relief that accompanied George W. Bush's departure from the White House, they remained shaken by a series of moves that Obama had made during the previous year to win over political moderates.

Instead of morphing into the socialist superhero that conservatives had feared and progressives had secretly longed for, Obama seemed intent on making political compromises that undermined the prospect of revolutionary change. Indeed, as his Cabinet appointments indicated, he appeared to be setting a course that would make him the second coming of Bill Clinton, but without the constant din of scandals.

The difference, though, was that this time the Left finally seemed willing, after decades of retreat, to perceive itself in terms of strength, rather than weakness. Instead of sitting back and letting the Republican Party once again shape the terms of political debate in the United States, organizations like MoveOn and its offshoots provided a basis for progressives to voice their concerns, both during the presidential campaign and in the wake of Obama's victory in November 2008.

The resurgence of the American Left as a significant political force can be attributed to a number of different factors, from rank-and-file progressives' greater familiarity with the networking possibilities opened up by the Internet, to the sharp economic downturn of Bush's second term. But the groundwork for that revitalization was laid in events like the discussion at the Rainbow Grocery, where progressives reacquainted themselves with the idea of collective action directed at goals distinct from the people undertaking it. And the impulse to intervene in world affairs at the local level, however unlikely to bring about major change, paralleled the rise of a new perspective on the United States' place in the world. Indeed, Obama's breakthrough speech at the 2004 Democratic Convention, in which he simultaneously embraced American small-town values and reminded his audience that they extend to places like

Kenya and Indonesia and to people with names like "Barack Obama," inspired many people who felt marginalized by the political process to see themselves once again as participants in it.

The way Obama told his story that night and at many occasions during his 2008 campaign—touching on his father's arrival in the United States from Africa, his Anglo mother's decision to spend much of her adult life abroad, and his Kansas grandmother's conformity to traditional stereotypes of the "real" America—resonated with people around the country (and the globe) precisely because it refused to flatten the complexity of his personal and political heritage into the timeworn templates of the White Republic. Even before he had staked out a position on the major issues of the election year in 2008, Obama had already positioned himself in a way that was in some respects more profound than any policy initiative could be.

This is what critics of Obama's supposed lack of substance, including his Democratic rival—and future secretary of state—Hillary Clinton, consistently failed to grasp. Obama had begun his campaign with the realization that Americans were as desperately in need of a way to circumvent their reflexes as their counterparts in Israel. In other words, he undertook the task of dismantling injurious conceptions of personal and political identity long before he set out to win the White House. His first book, published years before he became a significant political figure, represented an admirable attempt to set that process in motion. But it took Obama's rise to national prominence for his book's lessons to achieve critical mass in the American public.

The End of an Error

To an unprecedented degree, advances in technology (and their corresponding effects on various populations) have transformed the post–9/11 world into a place where the word "stability" sugests a failure to acknowledge the reality principle. Even while fundamentalists of all stripes strive to turn back the clock to a time when foundations were permanent instead of provisional, their own activism continues to further the demise of the world they sought to preserve. The massive economic upheavals of 2008 and 2009 indicate that this argument applies as well to the zealots who promote the unfettered market.

For countries like Israel and the United States of the post–9/11 years, this spells trouble. Single-minded devotion to a memory, as the slogan "Never again!" captures, or a vision, as in the Bush administration's Middle East policy, has consistently proved inadequate to the new era's political and economic circumstances. More and more, the present conjuncture demands flexibility incompatible with fixations. Indeed, provisional partnerships, with little chance of lasting as long as the special relationship between the Israel and the United States has, represent the chief source of hope for a better world. This is why the initiative shown by Nicolas Sarkozy to secure a ceasefire during Israel's incursion into Gaza in December 2008 could be regarded as a positive sign: an Israel less dependent on American approval is an Israel more likely to be persuaded to pursue a different political course. What nations like Israel and the United States need is a way to embrace the importance of finding new partners without sacrificing the strengths of their existing collaboration in the process.

A LEVANTINE SAN FRANCISCO

As I sat pondering my reluctance to make a public statement about Israel's sixtieth anniversary, I realized that my wariness of lapsing into clichés masked a deeper unease. As much as I loved my distant homeland, I recognized that its long-term commitment to both the United States and its own self-understanding had done more to diminish its achievements than anything else. The best aspects of Israeli society have developed not as a result of a fixation on the injury that legitimated the nation's establishment, but in times and places when the single-mindedness of "Never again!" was countered by the excitement of inventing new ways of living together in the shadow of history.

What I really wanted to do, on this significant day, was leave the collective narcissism of the celebration behind and find some provisional solidarity with other shawarma lovers. And that realization prompted me to acknowledge for the first time how thoroughly my exploration of what I'd taken to calling "Levantine San Francisco" had been implicated in the writing of this volume. All along, as I had sat poring over books and newspapers, feeling my stomach rumble or craving a cigarette, the better future for Israel I'd been working so hard to imagine could be discerned by walking around my old neighborhood, thousands of miles from the Middle East.

In retrospect, the most striking aspect of writing about my neighborhood in San Francisco was how neatly it paralleled what I was writing about Israel. What I had been struggling to articulate was the extent to which even the firm geographic distinctions that ground my sense of world affairs are being consistently called into question.

If *Ha'aretz* was publishing material as much for its followers in the Diaspora as for its domestic readership; if the staff at an alternative San Francisco grocery store was giving up its free time to discuss boycotting Israeli goods; if a movie about the "greatest Israeli soldier" encouraged Americans to identify with him in his struggle to make sense of life in the United States; if George W. Bush was using the occasion of a historic address at the Knesset to excoriate Barack Obama for failing to recognize that one doesn't negotiate with terrorists—if these examples and many others I have discussed throughout this book add up to one central premise, it is that making sense of the state of Israel today requires abandoning the conviction that we know where its boundaries lie.

This is not to underestimate the importance of resolving the territorial disputes resting at the center of the Israel-Palestine dispute. Certainly, the land matters, in some cases more than life itself. What we need to realize, however, is that confining our attention to the physical geography they concern cannot solve those arguments. The ways in which the plight of the Palestinians today eerily mirrors that of the Jews of yesterday are varied. But among the most revealing is that both Israel and Palestine have pushed traditional political cartography to the point of obsolescence. From the financial and political support that Israel has received from the Diaspora since its founding in 1948 to the microwarfare that the Mossad and Palestinian radicals waged throughout Europe in the 1970s, through the ways in which supporters of both nations continue to use them for polemical ends that have little to do with what happens in Gaza or Tel Aviv, their physical existence is impossible to confine to maps.

A GPS Unit Won't Help You Here

I saw four soldiers standing next to a table, rifles in hand, staring right back at us. They could have been Lebanese; they could have been something else. It was hard to tell from that distance. And their location at the southernmost entrance to Ghajar, a border village that had been divided between Israel and Lebanon until the war of 2006, did not help clarify matters. The town had been the site of numerous firefights over the years, including in 2005, when Hezbollah militiamen launched a combined infantry and rocket attack on IDF troops stationed there.

After the soldiers raised their rifles rather threateningly in our direction, we decided it was time to back out, turn around, and head up toward the Golan. Our destination was the Druze village of Majdal Shams, where we were hoping to arrive in time to see residents communicating via bullhorn with their Syrian cousins across the shouting wall. That was the border experience we'd had in mind for the day. The village is divided by a minefield from another Druze village, Hadar, on the Syrian side of the 1974 cease-fire line. It seemed like the perfect place to muse on the violence that abstract political divisions have done to these historic communities.

In our efforts to take a shortcut, though, we found

ourselves in the middle of a different shade of carto-
graphic anxiety. Driving out of Ghajar, an IDF Humvee
we'd passed by on the way into town had since parked
to set up a checkpoint. The soldiers manning it looked
distinctly unhappy about being there, peering at us
rather curiously, as though they were surprised to see
an Israeli-plated vehicle coming from the direction of
the Lebanese town. But they made no move to stop us,
and I issued a sigh of relief and waved goodbye.

When we returned home, I told a cousin about our
experience in Ghajar. "I thought the town was firmly
in our hands, and no longer divided," I began. "But the
second checkpoint we arrived at seemed like it was
manned by hostiles. The strange thing is that the flag
stretched out behind them was green, not yellow, like
Hezbollah's." My cousin frowned. "I'm very surprised
to hear this," he replied. "You should never have been
allowed to pass through that first checkpoint, let alone
get close to the second one. I'm going to make a phone
call. The commander responsible for this is going to get
into a lot of trouble."

While the fluid nature of the border in places like
Ghajar can be contrasted with the idea of "secure"
boundaries, the United States' own problems with its
southern border suggests that the only truly secure borders are ones which no one wants to cross or which
everybody can cross with equanimity. It takes a pretty
sturdy village to survive under those conditions, but
plenty of them have managed to do so, even in places
where multiple wars and countless smaller skirmishes
in between make their survival seem almost perverse.

We need those places, though, even the ones too

small to merit mention in news reports, because they are the only way we can figure out from afar what is going on during a time of crisis. Just as different military forces occupy those villages as a tactical maneuver, we capture them mentally as a way to secure our cognitive maps of an area.

THE RANGE OF FEAR

"They're extending their range of fire," my father said as soon as I answered my phone. "They finally managed to hit Afula." Almost a week into the 2006 Lebanon war, this was not reassuring news. "Well, Abba," I responded, trying to sound comforting, "that's still far from home."

What more could I say to my anguished father? With each missile fired at Israel's north, it was clear that the threat was slowly getting closer. "Well," my father said, clearing his throat, "our pilots are doing the best they can to knock these things out . . ."

I'd taken the day to work from home, and was standing in front of a local, Arab-owned convenience store as my father and I spoke about the situation. "Your family in Israel?" asked the clerk, overhearing the conversation. "Yes," I said, feeling a little uncomfortable. "They live in the north."

"My parents are under fire too," he said. "In a Christian town, just across the border." I asked him if he had been able to reach them. "Yes," he replied, sounding worried. "Apparently their power has been cut off, and they're running out of food. This puzzles me, because they are Christians, not Shia. Why are your people targeting us? It's stupid. We used to be your allies."

I went back to the store several times over the next few weeks, hoping to say hello again to the fellow and hear what ended up happening to his beleaguered family. But he had disappeared. Instead, I chatted several times with his replacement. A Christian from Bethlehem, he told me that he'd escaped to the United States during the siege of the city in May 2002. I wondered if his Lebanese colleague's parents were lucky enough to have done the same, and although I very much wanted to know, something kept me from inquiring. Considering that several rockets did eventually fall near my parents' home, I think I know why. More and more, I have learned to trust my instincts.

Ever since my frightening experience in Ghajar, I had kept wondering what the green flag near those four soldiers at the town's southern entrance had signified. I asked around on trips to Israel but could never get a firm answer. And then one day, as I was passing by that convenience store where I used to buy my cigarettes, I saw the same Lebanese clerk who had disappeared in the midst of the second Lebanon war.

Recognizing me, he extended his hand in greeting. We picked up right where our previous conversation had left off. "Did your family make it through?" I asked. "Yes," he answered, "barely . . . Your people bombed the hell out of their village." Right then, a young couple walked by us speaking Hebrew. I told him I was sorry before redirecting the conversation to a different topic.

Telling him about my experience in Ghajar, I asked if he could help me identify the puzzling green flag of the militiamen I'd run into there. He looked like someone patiently answering a neophyte's question. "Oh, they were Amal," he said, referring to the Lebanese Shia guerrilla organization that preceded Hezbollah. Even in San Francisco, his local knowledge of the area was stronger than that of the Israelis and Arabs I had queried in Israel.

NOT YOUR AVERAGE FALAFEL

Later, I mused on the calm with which the man had engaged me. Sure, he said *your people*. But it didn't feel like an indictment. The contrast with some of the self-righteous progressives I had argued with at the Rainbow Grocery and whom I had grown used to seeing during my food-related expeditions was striking. I recalled one incident that had particularly unnerved me.

Many well-meaning progressives end up epitomizing the reactionary caricature of the so-called "Israel Haters." Sometimes this can be chalked up to activists simply being inarticulate, employing self-incriminating terms like "the Jews" or "the Jewish lobby" that send conservatives in the Diaspora into a frenzy. Other times, though, it's hard to write the vitriol off as an unfortunate choice of words.

Standing in line at a Palestinian-owned restaurant in San Francisco's Mission District, an older woman wearing a fanny pack played with a set of keys hanging from her neck. Positioned in front of us, she was studying a Middle Eastern–looking gentleman to her right, whose accent revealed his nationality as soon as he began ordering his lunch. "One shawarma," he said, "im hummus." The cashier understood his Hebrew and smiled. The Israeli paid, gathered his food, and went to sit down.

Appearing a little flustered, the woman in front of us

was next, ordering her meal in a thick Scottish accent. Turning toward us as she walked back to her table, I could see she was wearing a T-shirt bearing a Palestinian flag, and that her eyes remained fixed on the Israeli. Whispering into my wife Jennifer's ear, I said, "Just wait. She's gonna go after that guy." Seating herself at a nearby table with a number of her friends, the woman did just that, opening with, "You Jews should be bloody ashamed at what you're doing in the Occupied Territories."

Looking up from his lunch, the Israeli groaned, "Please, I live here." Predictably, his response did nothing to staunch the flow of invective. "I just got back from spending six months in Hebron," she continued, her voice rising, "and it's obvious that you Jews want to impose an apartheid regime." Even though the Israeli made no response, staring at his food, she kept haranguing him, repeating the words "you Jews" as though it were a mantra. The Israeli picked up his food, slipped his headphones on, and left.

Lunch in Nazareth

The waiters placed course after course on the table without acknowledging us. Every time I would thank them for bringing us new dishes, or order an additional beverage for my wife, the waiters would avert their eyes. Quietly surveying the scene at our table, I wondered if something was amiss. Had one of us spilled food on our clothes? Had one of us been impolite to the maître d'? My father seemed unperturbed, chatting with a Christian friend who, together with his wife and daughter, had left his store several blocks away in order to have lunch with us. Seated at the opposite end of the table from me, our friend Françoise appeared to be happily engaged in conversation with my stepmother.

Despite how calm everyone appeared, something remained out of place. I could sense it in the stops and starts in my conversation with our Christian friend, who, having heard that I was journalist, asked me about my work, only to be interrupted by my father quietly signaling to save the topic for a later date. Obliging him, I would shift gears by pretending to have been surprised by a particularly tasty piece of food. "In all my years of coming to Nazareth," I said, "I've never had such good parsley salad."

Standing outside our friend's storefront, Françoise remarked how tense the atmosphere in the restaurant had been. "The air was so thick, you could cut it with a knife," she said as she took a drag on her cigarette. "These people are so obviously angry. And can you blame them? We leave them to the wolves, and yet they continue to show such graciousness toward us. And we don't deserve it."

Following Françoise's observations, I explained to Jennifer that two months before, at the height of the conflict, rockets fired by Hezbollah had reached this far south. "A couple of children were killed," I added, explaining that Nazareth's Arab neighborhoods lack bomb shelters. Looking shocked, Jennifer asked what an Israeli city was doing without such an obvious necessity. I could not give her an answer.

EQUALITY IS A CLICHÉ

Though it would be another eight months before I found out we were connected to one of the children killed that summer—hit while playing within feet of the home of the friend we'd shared that tense lunch with—our experience that day left an especially distinct impression on me. Despite the fact that a Palestinian Israeli colleague in the U.S. had sent me an e-mail telling me of the loss of his niece to Hezbollah fire during the war—the fourteen-year-old had also been struck by a missile—it was not until that moment, talking about the war in Nazareth, that I felt as though we shared something as members, whatever our differences, of the same community.

This epiphany was the result of a combination of factors: the increasing amount of time we'd spent going in and out of Nazareth over the past ten years, eating and shopping there, doing business with residents, and, unsurprisingly, making friends. But for most of this time—particularly since the fall 2000 riots in which twelve demonstrators had been shot dead by the police—Israeli Jews and Palestinians had never been more alienated from each other.

Yet I find it problematic to presuppose that harmony between Palestinians and Jews is somehow natural, as though all we must do is simply find a way to get back to this original state, either through ritual or through recognition that what ultimately unites us are shared values. Not only is this idea of a natural state of coexistence profoundly suspect, but even if it were to somehow be found valid, the pathways back to a harmonious golden age are permanently blocked. That period is usually presented as an abstract, precolonial era when Jewish and Muslim values were presumed to have been shared simply because they weren't in active conflict with each other.

Consequently, when the points of commonality are

restricted to the realm of supposed values, it becomes all too possible to mistake the "recognition of the other" for real social equality. One can invoke the fundamental equality of Arab and Jew under present-day Israeli law without acknowledging a very real hierarchy that emphasizes Jewish over Palestinian rights, even though no such prioritization is recognized by either official government rhetoric or by Israel's Basic Laws: "Arab and Jew are equals because Israel guarantees their equality, as long as Palestinian Israelis recognize the inherently Jewish cultural character of the state." Built into this logic is the unwritten rule that the state's Jewish character is inherently multicultural, and thus neither inspires nor tolerates discriminatory legislation that, for example, forbids the sale of public land to Palestinians or attempts to prohibit Arab parties from participating in national elections.

In the end, both liberal and conservative Jews enforce the second-class status of Palestinian Israelis, but they do so in entirely different ways. Despite the fact that they increasingly find themselves in fierce conflict with forces that want to make Israel even more Jewish, liberals nevertheless insist that the state maintain its Jewish character. On the flip side, because Palestinian Israelis have never accepted the idea of a Jewish state, conservatives consistently counter, Israel must always work to actively promote Jewish interests over those of its Palestinian citizens. Israel may still consider itself a democracy—one that has been forced to prosecute the Middle East equivalent of Jewish affirmative action to prevent Israeli Palestinians from taking advantage of their inalienable rights as citizens. The irony of this particular formulation is rich, recalling the white-men-are-discriminated-against rhetoric of American right-wing commentators during the initial efforts to repeal affirmative action in hiring and education.

For many critics of Israel's policies toward its domestic Palestinian population, a full withdrawal from the Occupied Territories will at best only complete half the work of peacemaking. At some point in the not-too-distant future, Israel will be forced to accommodate its Palestinian citizenry. Whether this will be accomplished by expanding the scope of Palestinian civil rights to precisely match those of Jewish Israelis—including requiring Palestinians to undertake the same set of civic responsibilities, such as compulsory military service—or through trying to ensure that the equal rights of Palestinians granted to them by Israel's Basic Laws cannot under any circumstances be compromised, the possibilities for improving their overall lot are numerous. And, quite frankly, there is a whole lot of improving that needs to be done.

BELGIUM, NOT BOSNIA

Since the events of October 2000, many Palestinian and Jewish Israelis have been exploring how such a discussion might be advanced. Pushed into gear by the remarkably high level of casualties sustained by Israel's Palestinian community during the second Lebanon war, the National Committee of the Heads of Arab Local Authorities, an organization consisting of forty of Israel's leading Palestinian activists, politicians, and academics, put forth a series of concrete proposals to deal with the situation in a December 2006 report entitled, "The Future Vision of the Palestinian Arabs in Israel." Detailed

in the now famous—or, to some, infamous—set of proposals, whose authors set out to examine the integration of Palestinians in Israeli society, the report centers
on a series of weighty, far-reaching recommendations
on how to remedy some of the structural disadvantages
that have reduced them to second-class citizens.

Contending that Israel's budget, land allocations,
laws, and state symbols discriminate against non-Jewish
citizens, the Future Vision document proposes that a
secular, "consensual" democracy of Arabs and Jews replace Israel's present form of government. Pointing to
Belgium's highly accommodating, multicultural policy
toward both its French- and Flemish-speaking citizens,
the Future Vision proposal advocates proportional representation and power sharing in place of Israel's present
parliamentary system, and cultural, linguistic, religious,
and educational autonomy for Israel's Palestinian citizenry. Additionally, the report recommends that Palestinian Israelis be considered an "indigenous" people
endowed with special collectively defined rights, along
the lines of the status of native peoples in countries like
Canada and the United States.

When the *New York Times* first broke the story of the
report in the United States the following February, correspondent Isabel Kershner was careful to note that nowhere in the Future Vision document was any mention
made of the situation in the West Bank and Gaza; the
report was only meant to address the status and future
of Palestinian citizens within Israel. Depending on how
one felt about the ultimate purpose of this report, it was
either a revolutionary exercise in undermining the raison d'être of the Jewish state, or a legitimate attempt to

find a way to ensure the peaceful and democratic continuity of that state into a necessarily modified future.

Predictably, Future Vision aroused a controversial
reception. Mailed to over thirty thousand households
in January 2007, the report achieved a kind of penetra-
tion that in previous years would have been unthinkable
for a Palestinian-authored political tract. The report's
frank discussion of the fate of the country's Palestinian
population, combined with its recommendations for the
country's future, spoke directly to Israel's contradic-
tions as an ethnic democracy. In its recommendations
for cultural autonomy in a proportionally representative
context, the report optimistically suggested, Israel's Palestinian and Jewish communities could have their kibbe
and eat it too.

In some ways, the most impressive aspect of the
Future Vision document was the audacity it exhibited
in proposing a comprehensive progressive direction for
the country, from its secular concept of citizenship to
its transformation of the Israeli legislature's makeup.
Coming on the heels of the new Labor Party's depressing retrenchment in the wake of the disastrous second
Lebanon war, such bold proposals struck many progressive Israelis, even those who strongly disagreed with
some of the report's recommendations, as a welcome
breath of fresh air. In terms of political imagination, Israel's Palestinians were the only community taking any
serious ideological initiative to reimagine the country.
Though they chose to request the elimination of certain
kinds of sacred cows fundamental to Israeli political
identity, such as the Law of Return, and identified Israel
as a project of colonial endeavors, the report's straight-

forward approach, refusing to worry about the country's hardened political reflexes, got through to Israelis eager to break new ground in moving the country forward.

In the plethora of Jewish responses that followed Future Vision's publication, both liberals and conservatives found themselves taken aback by its recommendations. Former *Jerusalem Post* editor Amotz Asa-El waxed angrily in a Jewish Telegraphic Agency op-ed about the document's confirmation of the Israeli Palestinian insistence on two states. In *Moment*, the Jewish American bimonthly, *Forward* staff writer Nathan Gutmann articulated the more flexible position that everything the report was asking for was reasonable and ought to be taken seriously, with the exception of the plan to evolve into a non-Jewish state.

For many Jewish progressives, Future Vision represented a positive vision for Israel, though one that went further than they were comfortable with. Although the Israeli Left has repeatedly sought to improve the situation of the country's Palestinian population over the years, it has more often than not stopped short of advocating the creation of a multiethnic democracy in the place of a Jewish state. While one may understand this hesitancy, the fact remains that Future Vision helped to further problematize this inhibition by defining what kind of state it would take to ultimately grant Israel's non-Jewish citizenry real social equality.

If this portrait of Israel resembles the secular, binational state sought by the Palestine Liberation Organization during the 1970s, then it is the fault of Israel for not developing a sufficient conception of citizenship and government, within a Jewish context, that could contain such a desire for all of its citizens. Though it remains highly unlikely that any secular democracy designed along Belgian lines will ever be formally accepted by Israel, in principle the report's ideas are worthy, and cannot be attributed to any pernicious or scheming revolutionary mindset. The fact that some regard it as such is distressing, because, irrespective of the Palestinian question, the guiding principles of the political system the report proposes would ultimately be better for Israelis as well.

ISRAEL AS A VOCATION

I don't want to end this book, undertaken in the spirit of indicating how the prospect of a better Israel is more than a utopian fantasy, on such a negative note. But the paralysis demonstrated by the nation's political echelon in recent years makes it difficult to see much hope for significant change in the immediate future.

This is another reason why I ultimately couldn't write anything substantive about Israel's sixtieth birthday. I think about the country constantly. But I realized that I am not sentimental about its political existence the way I am, for example, about its cuisine. It was a liberating insight, one that made me feel better about the trip my wife and I were going to take to Israel the following month. I knew that the visit would differ little from our previous trips to see my father and his family. The nation's birthday mattered less to me than my own. My investment in the place did not need to be legitimated by going through the motions of an ultimately empty ritual.

Of course, like the pundits I read religiously, I could have marked the occasion by providing my own interpretation of Israel's Italian-style political scene and the potential I see for a Berlusconi-equivalent to take the reigns of government. Or I could have talked about the remarkable films I had just seen at the San Francisco International Film Festival, such as *Vasermil*, *Children of the Sun*, or the Israeli-directed *Under the Bombs*, which, like *Walk on Water* and *Paradise Now* before it, offers American audiences a wholly unfamiliar point of view: that of an upper-class Lebanese mother touring her devastated homeland in a taxi during the 2006 war, looking for her dead son. At some point, I reasoned, I would eventually do both things.

For the anniversary itself, however, such writing would still have felt too much like commemoration. I reached the conclusion, in writing about my inability to write on the subject, that I am perfectly fine with the idea that Israel functions as a vocation for me. It calls me to thought and action, every day of the year, without ever diminishing my workload. This particular job takes a lot of energy. Adding to the strain by forcing myself to take a position on its birthday would have been overwhelming.

THE GIFT ECONOMY

But I did start thinking of a different anniversary commemoration: on June 5, 2007, though I'd had no plans to formally mark the fortieth anniversary of the Six-Day War, I found myself doing the opposite of what most Israelis did that day: eating lunch at the home of my Christian friend in Nazareth.

The meal began with a parsley salad, followed by a plate of lamb-filled lasagna. In between, the hostess served her own homemade kibbe, followed by a main course of roast beef and baked potatoes. Dessert was doled out in three stages: fresh fruit, followed by a cornmeal-based crème caramel, and then a mix of pistachio ice cream and lime sorbet.

Even though we all knew each other fairly well, for some reason the atmosphere was somewhat uneasy. Long moments of silence were followed by bilingual bursts of nervous conversation in Hebrew and English. Everything felt forced. In this context, the immense quantities of rich food served their purpose, bludgeoning all of those in attendance with their heaviness.

It was only after the meal that talk turned to politics. Using my visiting American friend Vance's presence as a pretext to discuss the situation in Iraq, our host expressed enormous frustration with the United States' strategy in the region under the Bush administration. Though I couldn't quite hear the specifics of our host's complaints across the table, I could see his elbows jerking right and left.

Then our hostess captured my attention. "This is for your wife," she said. Handing me a box of perfume with the word *Poison* written on it, she told me how beautiful she found Jennifer, and how much she admired her extremely short, punkish bleached hair. "She's very courageous to wear it like that. Please give her my warmest regards."

Later that day, as I was driving down to the Basilica of the Annunciation to take Vance on a tour of the Christian holy site, I received a call on my mobile from an American Jew, a magazine editor then based in Jerusalem, who wanted me to replace the term "Occupied Territories" in an article I was editing for him with "Disputed Territories." The timing of his request stunned me.

I wanted to tell the editor that I was in Nazareth,

spending the day with Arab friends. But I didn't. Not because I feared his reaction; I couldn't have cared less. What held me back was my desire to have my experiences of this day somehow pass unnoticed, as though it were all routine, not an exception to the otherwise cruel rule of the last four decades of Israeli history.

When I returned to the United States, I called my friend Charlie to tell him of my mixed feelings about this anti-anniversary celebration. "Well, perfume is nice," he said, "but what kind was it?"

I laughed. "Poison. It was Poison."

Charlie shrieked with glee. "You're kidding! That's the best bilingual pun ever."

I didn't get it. "You mean in Hebrew?"

"Not Hebrew. Do I know Hebrew, Joel? I was thinking of German."

I remained confused.

"Didn't you ever see photos of the Zyklon B canisters from Auschwitz?"

Yes, I had.

"Printed above the skull-and-crossbones symbol is the word *Giftgas*. The German word for poison is *Gift*. Talk about giving the gift of irony!"

I smiled. There are many Jews who recoil at the very idea of Holocaust humor. But I regard it as a more powerful testament to my people's strength than all the IDF's military victories. I thought about the people I liked conversing with at my favorite Middle Eastern restaurants and markets in San Francisco. I knew that this was the sort of tale they could appreciate. Maybe we could share a laugh together. And some hummus.

Also available from Akashic Books

JERUSALEM CALLING
A Homeless Conscience in a Post-Everything World
by Joel Schalit
216 pages, trade paperback original, $14.95

"This remarkable collection of essays by an astute young writer covers a wide range of topics . . . [and] provides an overview of contemporary critical, radical thinking . . . This is the debut of a new and original thinker." —*Publishers Weekly*, starred review

"Joel Schalit is part of a new generation of secular Jewish leftists who issue a challenge to state-authorized religion in Israel and throughout the world. With his political autobiography, Schalit reveals the reactionary ideas that drive today's liberal rhetoric. He also makes a passionate case for ending military violence, which rips apart countries and families alike." —*San Francisco Bay Guardian*

OF MULE AND MAN
by Mike Farrell
224 pages, trade paperback original, $15.95

"*Of Mule and Man* is a one-of-a-kind American road trip . . . Farrell travels through both the beautiful and busted landscape from desert to bayou, urban to rural, listening in and arguing silently with conservative talk radio found in even the most remote places, and ending each day at bookstores and community organizations to have conversations with activists, friends, and family who are doing the hard work of social justice in every neighborhood. 'Heroes abound in this world,' Farrell writes. He is one of them." —Walter Mosley, author of *The Tempest Tales*

JUST CALL ME MIKE
A Journey to Actor and Activist
by Mike Farrell
378 pages, trade paperback, $16.95
*A *Los Angeles Times* best seller

"I've always just called him Mike. But now I have to call him talented, brave, principled, indefatigable, thoughtful, generous, and a man driven by his conscience. I learned things about him in this book I never knew before. So now I have to call him humble, too. He's really kind of irritating." —Alan Alda

"A simply told, extraordinary story." —*Los Angeles Free Press*

BORN ON THE FOURTH OF JULY
by Ron Kovic
228 pages, trade paperback, $14.95

"[T]he most personal and honest testament published thus far by any young man who fought in the Vietnam War . . . Classic and timeless."
—*New York Times*

"Extraordinarily effective . . . Kovic's unabashed expression of feelings . . . becomes a form of bravery."
—*Newsweek*

WE OWE YOU NOTHING: PUNK PLANET
The Collected Interviews (Expanded Edition)
edited by Daniel Sinker
402 pages, trade paperback, $17.95

"This collection of Q&As consistently engages . . . and successfully functions as a detailed document of the tight-knit modern-day punk community." —*Entertainment Weekly*

"All of the interviews are probing and well thought out, the questions going deeper than most magazines would ever dare; and each has a succinct, informative introduction for readers who are unfamiliar with the subject. Required reading for all music fans."
—*Library Journal*

THE PATH TO GENEVA
The Quest for a Permanent Agreement, 1996–2004
by Yossi Beilin
380 pages, hardcover original, $22.95

"Beilin's recollections should be required reading for anyone interested in the search for peace in the Middle East."
—Jimmy Carter

"[Path] shows that civil society in Israel and the West Bank is still alive and refuses to give into pessimism."
—Thomas L. Friedman, *New York Times*

These books are available at local bookstores.
They can also be purchased online through www.akashicbooks.com.
To order by mail send a check or money order to:

AKASHIC BOOKS
PO Box 1456, New York, NY 10009
www.akashicbooks.com, info@akashicbooks.com

(Prices include shipping. Outside the U.S., add $12 to each book ordered.)